This Little Light *of Mine*

This Little Light of Mine

A WOMAN WITH DOWN SYNDROME SHINES BRIGHTLY IN THE WORLD.

ROSEMARY HEDDENS
With words from
KIRSTIN HEDDENS

WestBow
PRESS
A DIVISION OF THOMAS NELSON

Copyright © 2012 by Rosemary Heddens.

All rights reserved. No part of this book may be used or reproduced by any means, graphic, electronic, or mechanical, including photocopying, recording, taping or by any information storage retrieval system without the written permission of the publisher except in the case of brief quotations embodied in critical articles and reviews.

WestBow Press books may be ordered through booksellers or by contacting:

WestBow Press
A Division of Thomas Nelson
1663 Liberty Drive
Bloomington, IN 47403
www.westbowpress.com
1-(866) 928-1240

Because of the dynamic nature of the Internet, any web addresses or links contained in this book may have changed since publication and may no longer be valid. The views expressed in this work are solely those of the author and do not necessarily reflect the views of the publisher, and the publisher hereby disclaims any responsibility for them.

Any people depicted in stock imagery provided by Thinkstock are models, and such images are being used for illustrative purposes only.

Certain stock imagery © Thinkstock.

ISBN: 978-1-4497-6090-8 (sc)
ISBN: 978-1-4497-6089-2 (hc)
ISBN: 978-1-4497-6085-4 (e)

Library of Congress Control Number: 2012913190

Printed in the United States of America

WestBow Press rev. date: 7/31/2012

*To Craig and Michael,
who share our story*

Contents

Preface ix
Acknowledgments xiii

1. "You Have a Little Girl." 1
2. A Whole New World 11
3. Getting Schooled 22
4. Living with Bratinella 33
5. "One, We Are the Girls!" 43
6. Teaching the Teacher 55
7. The Not Too Easy Reader 74
8. On to Higher Learning 95
9. All the World's a Stage 106
10. Working Girl 118
11. Driving Me Crazy 131
12. How Can Our Nest Be Empty? 142
13. Modern Problems 153
14. Angels Among Us 166

Bibliography 177
About the Authors 179

Preface

"Timing is everything," as the expression goes. When I gave birth in 1975 to a daughter with Down syndrome, I had no idea how significant my timing was. When Kirstin began preschool at the age of one, her teacher told me I could not have chosen a better time to have a child with a disability. It was years later, when I began taking courses to become a special education teacher, that I came to understand what she meant. In 1975, Congress passed Public Law 94-142, which established special education for all school-age children with disabilities. Special education has changed a great deal since the early days. For example, it now reaches down into preschool, giving special students a jump-start. But we had to pay for Kirstin's special preschool program, which was quite a sacrifice for young parents. I am so happy that parents today don't have to bear that burden.

I guess you could say that Kirstin and special education have grown up together. She is the product of a school system that had to provide a free, appropriate public education for her and all children with or without special challenges. How well has special education worked? You be the judge as you get to know Kirstin. But this is not just the story of special education; it is the story of a special woman. Kirstin's amazing accomplishments make her worthy of having her story told, and so we are telling it together. Kirstin has her own comments to make, and in every chapter, she has the final words. She decided to name her section "Kirstin's Side of the Story." I'm sure you will find it enlightening and inspiring.

Most authors are worried about getting the approval of an editor or critics or the readers themselves. Before I even get that far, I have to get my words past a more severe judge. I don't have the luxury of making things sound better than they are. I won't be embellishing stories to get a laugh. Everything I write must be honest and respectful. Kirstin will hold me to that—a fact I learned the hard way.

When Kirstin was two years old, I was the chairman of Mother's March for March of Dimes in Chandler, Arizona. The local newspaper sent a reporter to our home to interview me. She asked a lot of questions about raising a special needs child and about what I thought life would be like for us in the future. She took a nice picture of Kirstin and me, sitting on the swings in our backyard.

I had totally forgotten about the experience when, many years later, my cousin, Connie, came across her copy of the article and sent it to me. We were living in Chino Valley, Arizona, by that time, and Kirstin was in high school. Without looking at the article, I passed it to Kirstin, thinking she would enjoy reading it. Several days went by, and Kirstin never said a word about the article. Finally I asked her what she thought about it. After a few awkward moments, she muttered, "I was embarrassed." Puzzled by her response, I took a look at the article myself. To my horror, I discovered that I had painted a pretty dreary future for our family. I had said that Kirstin would stay with us no matter what; we would never put her in an institution. Even though it might be embarrassing at times, we would keep her with us wherever we went.

The person I was picturing back then had no resemblance to the bright, charismatic charmer who is the adult Kirstin. Had I considered that someday Kirstin would be capable not only of reading the article but of fully understanding what she read, I would never have spoken those words.

Before Kirstin's birth, I had practically no experience with special needs children. In high school, I had read *Angels Unaware,* written by Dale Evans, which is about her daughter, who had Down syndrome. She and Roy Rogers raised this daughter at home. It was written from the point of view of the child, who only lived for two years. It greatly moved me, but I never considered that someday I would be the parent of another angel. At the time Dale Evans had her child, parents were being encouraged to put their disabled children in institutions. In fact, in her book, she talks about the institutions being so full that children were placed in foster homes until they could be institutionalized. Doctors told parents it was in the best interest of the family. The special child would be a financial drain and take up so much of the parents' time that their other children would suffer.

When Kirstin was diagnosed with Down syndrome, the doctor mentioned putting her in an institution as a possibility, but it was not one we ever considered. Nor was it something the doctor expected us to consider. Parents today aren't given that option at all, because such institutions don't exist. If families are unable to care for their special needs children, there are generous, loving families eager to adopt. At times, excellent foster families provide appropriate homes where these special children are able to thrive. Adults with special needs remain at home or in group homes as participating members of their communities. This is also the story of how that came about.

I chose to call our book *This Little Light of Mine*, thinking of the Sunday school song, "This little light of mine, I'm gonna let it shine . . . Hide it under a bushel? No! I'm gonna let it shine."

Kirstin does shine in this world. Because she was able to attend school with her peers, students today don't say, as I did, their experience with special needs children is limited to reading a book. These special students are their friends and classmates. Later in life, they are their customers, employees, and coworkers, and all our lives are better for it. While they do have special needs, they also have special gifts. There is plenty they can teach us in this cynical, dog-eat-dog world. From them we can learn tolerance and patience, which are virtues most of us are weak in. Yes, Kirstin does shine in the world, and she lights it up everywhere she goes.

Rosemary Heddens

KIRSTIN'S SIDE OF THE STORY

Everyone is special in his or her own way. I do think about special needs children like me. We like to help people. I have lots of friends with disabilities. I have friends at work who care about me. My parents help me with my problems and make me happy. I enjoy reading in my leisure. I hope you enjoy reading my book.

Kirstin Heddens

Acknowledgments

As this is my first large writing project, I feel fortunate to have the very capable staff at WestBow Press to guide and assist me. They have treated me as a professional, offering suggestions and valuing my opinion. I couldn't imagine going through this process without them.

I would also like to thank my family and friends who have offered so much support. My son, Michael, who took our picture for the back cover, has helped me remember some of the stories. I especially want to thank Vikki Heim and Katie Creech, whose enthusiasm has kept me going. My support staff at school—Linda Brown, Linda Vetter, and Janet Hill—were kind enough to read my early efforts and encourage me to continue. My grandchildren—Christopher, Brenna, and Avery—as well as my mother, Lorene, have been a great source of support.

I must thank my husband and best friend, Craig, who has been there with me through my tears, fears, and frustrations as well as the lighthearted moments reliving our funny stories. I certainly can't forget my daughter, Kirstin, without whom this book wouldn't even be possible. Through it all, she has reminded me, "You can do it."

Finally, I thank my Lord and Savior, Jesus Christ, who has begun a good work in me and will continue it.

See that you do not despise one of these little ones, for I say to you that their angels in heaven always look upon the face of my heavenly Father.   Matthew 18:10

(From The New American Bible. The New Catholic Translation. Catholic Bible Press. Copyright 1987 by Thomas Nelson, Inc.)

Chapter One
෩෪
"You Have a Little Girl."

"You have a little girl." Those were the first words I heard from the nurse when I woke up in the recovery room on June 9, 1975, after a cesarean section. Realizing through the fog of anesthesia that I had gotten what I wanted, I closed my eyes and went back to sleep. Later, back in my room, the doctor came in to tell me all had gone well. My baby was slightly jaundiced but otherwise fine. He mentioned her ear was kind of floppy, but he said it would probably be all right later. If not, a few stitches would fix it. No problem.

When the nurse brought my daughter to me, I checked her over, of course, counting fingers and toes. My husband, Craig, and our son, Michael, came to visit. They had already named her Kirstin, after one of Michael's friends at preschool. I added the middle name, Renee, as it was the name of one of my cousins, and I had always admired it. Later, my mom and Craig's parents came in to see me. There are three boys in Craig's family, so his mother, Mary, was especially pleased to have a little girl. She told me that when the nurse said it was a girl, she thought she was talking to someone else. We all laughed at that and were happy we had the healthy baby girl we wanted.

I stayed in the hospital for three days, recovering from the surgery and getting to know my new daughter. I couldn't quite figure out who she looked like, and sometimes when we were alone, I would whisper, "Who are you?" I don't know what made me feel that way, but there just seemed to be something different about this new addition to our family. Her hospital photo might have provided some clues, but I sent those back to the photographer with a note saying that they weren't very flattering. Later, when we were home, Craig, a professional photographer, took some very nice baby pictures. That made up for the ugly ones from the hospital photographer.

I had tried breast-feeding with Michael and had not been too successful. My doctor wasn't very encouraging, but I wanted to try again anyway. The doctor gave me a formula just in case. Kirstin seemed to catch on to the breast-feeding, so mother and daughter were doing fine.

At home, Kirstin grew slowly. I wrote in her baby book that she was very strong from birth, and at three weeks she was able to turn from her stomach to her back with some struggling. At four weeks she was able to lift her chest a short distance when placed on her stomach. Kirstin was very flexible, even for a baby. She was alert, happy, and by two months, she recognized her mother and father. She seemed to be hitting the major milestones for her age. She laughed and made noises and played. There were some spaces in her baby book that I never filled in. Those were the spaces that asked for the age when she first "Objected noisily when a toy was taken from her," and "Showed her temper when something didn't suit her." Kirstin was a very agreeable child from the start.

Our major concern with Kirstin's development was her size. She seemed to be adding weight very slowly. At birth she weighed six pounds six ounces, but by eight months, she only weighed about nine pounds. She grew so slowly that she is probably one of the few babies who actually wore out her infant clothes before she grew out of them. At first the doctor didn't seem too concerned, but when Kirstin was about eight months old, I had her in for a routine visit. The doctor became almost angry and told me that my baby was not being properly nourished. He sat her up, and though she didn't fall over, she wobbled quite a bit. That too, according to the doctor, was a sign that she wasn't getting enough food. I was still trying to breast-feed, but I had also attempted to give Kirstin a bottle. She never quite caught on to the bottle but was drinking fine out of a cup and eating lots of baby food. As I drove home, the doctor's words rang in my ears. How could I have neglected my daughter and allowed this to happen? Filled with guilt I cried during most of the forty-five-minute drive from Phoenix to Chandler.

After I had a few days to recover and be consoled by my loving husband, I decided to seek another opinion. After all, Kirstin's doctor was not a pediatrician; he was our family doctor. A few weeks later, I made an appointment with a pediatrician in Tempe and took Kirstin for her first visit. He examined her and assured me that she was not suffering from malnutrition but was just a very small person. He had me gather information about the members of both sides of Kirstin's family tree, their heights and so on. From this information, he concluded that she was inherently small, and there was nothing to worry about.

This news gave us great relief, of course, and Kirstin did put on a few pounds. But as she approached her first birthday, she had not yet started crawling. Kirstin was pulling herself up and walking around tables, which made us think maybe she was going to skip the crawling stage. Still, concerns about her size and development lingered in the back of my mind. Kirstin was very flexible and could actually fold in half. She liked to sleep with her legs spread apart and her head down between her legs. When she sat up, she started from that same position and used her hands to push herself up. I had never seen another baby do that.

At eleven months, Kirstin came down with strep throat. Her pediatrician prescribed antibiotics and said she should be better in a few days. Kirstin continued to be sick and was crying a lot, something that was not like her. Repeated calls to the doctor got responses such as, "She probably has a virus along with the strep throat. It will take longer for the virus to go away." After a week, I decided that something had to be done, so I took her to the clinic in Chandler. A doctor there examined her and said he didn't know what was wrong, but she was dehydrated and needed to be in the hospital.

Kirstin was admitted to the hospital while her pediatrician was out of town. A doctor who was taking his calls came in to examine her. He felt of her soft spot and ordered a spinal tap. As the day wore on, more and more of our family members came to the hospital for the vigil wait for information. I remember my mother-in-law, Mary, looked in the chapel first and was relieved to find I wasn't there. Her hope was that things weren't as bad as first reported.

The spinal tap confirmed meningitis caused by the strep bacteria. Kirstin was very, very ill. The doctor explained that she would need to receive antibiotics through a drip for ten days. There was a possibility of death, and if she lived, there could be residual affects such as mental retardation.

I will never forget watching as three adults tried to hold down an eleven-pound baby, kicking and screaming, to do the IV cutdowns. They were amazed that such a small child could be so strong. Kirstin still has the scars on her feet from those cutdowns.

For the next ten days, my life was at the hospital. The baby food the hospital provided was not what Kirstin was eating at home. So I brought in foods she was familiar with. I fed her, bathed her, and changed her as if she were at home. Not trusting that she would be cared for adequately in the busy hospital, I didn't leave her side until after she was asleep for the night. Early the next morning, I was there to care for her again. If the mother-daughter bond hadn't been formed before that, it was cemented now.

Kirstin made a full recovery from the meningitis with no obvious ill effects. Developmentally she was where she had been. Before the meningitis, she had a small vocabulary of four words: "bye-bye," "baby," "Momma," "Dada." She hadn't lost any ground it seemed. Still, her size was a concern, so I asked our new pediatrician (I sent the other one packing) if he could run some tests to find out why she was not growing any faster. I remember he wrote on the order, "failure to thrive," as the reason for the tests. This brought back old memories of Kirstin's first doctor, who told me I was not feeding her properly. Nevertheless, I wanted to know if something was wrong, even if it was my fault.

When the test results were in, the doctor called us into his office. I can remember this like it was yesterday. On a little piece of paper he had written the word "mongoloid." He slid the paper across his desk to us and asked if we knew what it was. Craig said he did not, but I told the doctor I thought I did know. Then he explained to us that "mongoloid" was a term that was not being used anymore. What Kirstin has is a chromosome defect called Down syndrome. The next part of his explanation was kind of a blur: "extra chromosomes" . . . "happens at conception" . . . "in every cell of her body." He showed us a printout of some wavy Xs and pointed to the one labeled 21. Here was the problem it seemed. Kirstin has three instead of two. It was hard to focus on what he was telling us as the shock was setting in, but I do remember something very important he said. He told us to read as much as we could about Down syndrome. "Everything you read is true," he said, "but it won't necessarily be true about your child."

Craig and I said very little to each other on the way home. It took a few days for the shock to lessen slightly. Then we had the difficult task of telling our family and friends. Most of them were supportive and encouraging, which was what we needed. Our friends reminded us that we still had a healthy, happy baby. Nothing had really changed except we now knew more about her possible future than most parents learn at such an early age.

I also received calls from Pilot Parents, a nonprofit group that assists parents of children with special needs by providing support and answers to questions. Someone from the Down's Syndrome Association called me as well. These calls helped me know that we were not alone—or the first parents to ever have to deal with this. I'm not sure how we would have gotten through those early days without the support we received. Of course, our faith in God helped bring us through. We were sure that He wouldn't give us this challenge without being there to help us every step of the way.

There were a few well-meaning friends whose pity we could have done without. They went on and on about what a tragedy it was. I almost felt it necessary to defend my daughter as not being some kind of heinous creature. She wasn't Rosemary's baby. Well yes, she was, but not *that* Rosemary's baby. Nothing had really changed. Kirstin was still the same baby we had before we knew she had Down syndrome. She was still small and somewhat delayed, but now we knew why.

Psychiatrist Elisabeth Kübler-Ross identified five stages of grief: denial, anger, bargaining, depression, and acceptance. I remember going through three of those stages. The first stage, denial, was a period of shock and disbelief. We had been told so many times by so many doctors that Kirstin was fine, we were not really prepared for such a diagnosis. We had been thinking that maybe Kirstin had some digestive problems or food allergies that could be easily fixed. Now we were being told that our daughter's life and our lives were about to drastically change. How could we possibly take it all in?

Denial didn't really last too long, because the evidence was so conclusive. There was no room for doubt when we were shown Kirstin's chromosome karyotype. There were obviously three twenty-first chromosomes. The doctor explained that there is a type of Down syndrome called mosaic. This type happens after the first cell division, so not every cell has the extra chromosome. The effects are less pervasive, and children with the mosaic form usually function at a higher level. He assured us though, that enough cells had been sampled to rule out the mosaic form.

After the denial stage, I moved into the anger stage. Craig was fortunate enough to avoid this stage. He had a job to keep him busy. I, on the other hand, was at home with the children. Michael started kindergarten, and that left me and Kirstin. I remember being in a store, pushing her in the stroller, and seeing other moms with their babies. I instantly hated them and wished them an unhappy future, complete with some tragedy for their prefect babies. *Why did this happen to me?* I wanted to know. All my life I had eaten properly, and I never took drugs. I didn't even drink coffee. This was just so unfair.

I imagine that any parent on finding out that her child has a serious problem would ask, "Why me?" If Kirstin had cancer, juvenile diabetes, or a physical disability, I'm sure I would have reacted in a similar way. I'm also sure that what brings parents out of that stage is activity, finding out what can be done. And so it was for us. Shortly after Kirstin's first birthday, we enrolled her in an early intervention program. We were doing something about her disability, and that made all the difference. We skipped the next two stages of grief and found ourselves accepting and even enjoying our new role as Kirstin's parents.

Eventually life goes on, and so it did in our case. In later years, I came to realize how fortunate I was to skip the depression stage and the guilt it creates. I have met other parents who did go through the guilt stage, and some who never left it. Guilt is the last thing a parent needs when dealing with a special child. In an attempt to assuage their guilt, I have seen parents shower attention on, spoil, and otherwise make their child more difficult to live with.

For the first year of her life, we treated Kirstin as if she had no problems, because we didn't know any differently. That fact had a profound affect on our attitude toward our daughter. When I was pregnant with Michael, I read Doctor Spock's baby book. It seemed like Michael had read it too, because he hit every milestone almost on the dot. If Dr. Spock said he should have two teeth at six months, almost to the day, the teeth popped in his mouth. When Kirstin came along, I expected the same progress. I'll never forget my tiny daughter sitting in the grocery cart, holding on for dear life as I wheeled her through the store. More than once someone stopped to ask if she wasn't too little to be sitting in the cart that way. I shot back, "She's nine months old!" At nine months, her brother was sitting in the grocery cart with no problem. I hadn't any reason to think Kirstin should not be able to do the same.

By the time we knew Kirstin had Down syndrome, it was too late to start thinking of her as a child with a disability. I've always been grateful for that year. Most parents learn at birth and sometimes even sooner. I'll never know what that is like. Would we have done things differently had we known? Most likely we would have. Would it have been better for Kirstin? I'm not so sure. I have read horror stories of how doctors told parents to institutionalize their baby because he would never sit up, crawl, walk, or talk. Kirstin was already doing most of those things, so our doctor would have been wasting his time telling us that. Instead, he told us that Kirstin would do everything all the other children were able to do; she would just do it a little later.

Taking the doctor's advice, I did go to the library to read as much as I could find about Down syndrome. Everything I read said pretty much the same thing. There are developmental delays ranging from mild to moderate. Kirstin's fell into the mild range. She was sitting alone pretty well by ten months, crawling by thirteen months, and walking by eighteen months. Kirstin developed verbal skills at a more normal rate. She was using a few words by age one and putting words together by two and a half. Before she was four years old, she was speaking in sentences. Kirstin had articulation problems, but these improved after she had her tonsils out, her palate spread, and orthodontics to straighten her teeth. It was quite a challenge, but we found an excellent orthodontist who worked miracles. Today, Kirstin's speech is very intelligible, especially to those who know her well. She likes to talk fast and use all of her excellent vocabulary, struggling sometimes to pronounce the big words she knows.

I have never heard or read of another instance where doctors failed to diagnose Down syndrome at birth. Kirstin managed to fool three doctors who have been trained to identify Down syndrome, and she fooled them for an entire year! In their defense, I must say that every psychological evaluation written about Kirstin begins with a statement like this one from her first psychologist's report: "Her facies are not typical of the vast majority of Downs children and her abilities appear to be at a higher level than the typical Downs child."

When doctors fail to identify a condition that they should have been aware of, the doctor who discovers it is required to notify the other doctors. By the time I returned to my gynecologist for a one-year checkup, he had received a letter from Kirstin's pediatrician. He asked me if, in fact, my baby had Down syndrome, and I assured him she did. He still found it hard to believe.

Kirstin has the typical Down syndrome features, but they are less pronounced. Her muscle tone is a little low, but she has always been amazingly strong. Kirstin does have some of the problems associated with Down syndrome. She wears glasses for strabismus and had vent tubes inserted in her ears five times. She still doesn't hear well if you are speaking to her from behind. Heart issues are common, and Kirstin has a cleft valve that causes a heart murmur. No restrictions have been recommended by her doctors, but they do monitor the condition of her valve. Many people with Down syndrome are overweight. At four feet ten inches, Kirstin's weight of 106 pounds seems just fine. She is the one who watches what she eats and stays active to keep in shape. All things considered in that genetic roll of the dice, Kirstin came out pretty lucky.

When Kirstin was three years old, her preschool teacher gave me a book to read. It was written by two psychologists who had a child with Down syndrome. They talked about how they placed his crib in just the right spot so that he would receive the most stimulation. Everything about his day was calculated to provide the best environment for him to develop properly. I thought about how we hadn't done any of those things. When she was a newborn, we didn't even know we should be doing them. Now she was three years old. Was it too late? When I reached the part about their son starting to walk at age three, I looked up at Kirstin. She was spinning around the driveway on her Big Wheel, happy and engaged in what she was doing. Maybe we hadn't done everything just right, but we were doing okay.

As with all situations we find ourselves in, there are blessings to go along with the challenges. While those with Down syndrome require special help, they also provide their families with special joy. I've heard it suggested that instead of Down syndrome, it should be called Up syndrome. Kirstin smiles most of the time and sees the bright side of every situation. She has the ability to spread happiness wherever she goes; it's contagious. Her concern for others is genuine. There is not a phony, conniving, or distrustful bone in her body. This makes her more vulnerable, but it also makes her a beautiful example of how the rest of us should live.

A doctor can explain exactly how Down syndrome occurs, and I can understand and accept what he tells me. Still I do not believe it is a mistake of nature. God does not make mistakes. Kirstin is as she was intended to be. God has a purpose and plan for her, as He does for all His children. He sees her not as the world sees her but as His perfect creation.

KIRSTIN'S SIDE OF THE STORY

My mom asked me to tell you how I feel about having Down syndrome. I feel like I'm happy about it. I do have a problem with my knee. One good thing is being able to wear glasses, so I can see and do some reading. I feel I am special in my own way. I have some friends with Down syndrome. We do look a lot like each other, as if we are people who are related. Sometimes people call me by the wrong name. They think I am someone else with Down syndrome. I just go along with it, because I don't want to hurt their feelings. That's not my style. I would like people to remember that even though we look alike, we are all unique.

Chapter Two

৪০০৪

A Whole New World

*I*n the summer of 1976, Kirstin was enrolled at the Marc Center preschool in Mesa at the ripe old age of thirteen months. I couldn't imagine what she would do in school at that age. She wasn't even walking yet. Kirstin had a speech therapist, physical therapist, and an occupational therapist. She was hardly talking, and I didn't think she was ready for a job. This seemed like a lot of therapy for such a small child.

Kirstin was in what is called an infant stimulation program. Each therapist contributed goals to Kirstin's Individual Program Plan (IPP). Her preschool teacher was responsible for helping Kirstin work on her goals on a daily basis. As part of her therapy, Kirstin received vestibular stimulation intended to help her nervous system develop more fully. One of the activities involved placing Kirstin on a swing. Her teacher would rotate the swing around and around until the chain was wound up. Then she would let go of the swing, allowing it to unwind. In another activity, Kirstin was placed over a large ball and rolled forward so that she would put her hands down to catch herself from falling. This helped develop her reflexes.

Flo Smith, Kirstin's preschool teacher, was truly devoted to her work. She showed genuine love for Kirstin and all the children in her class. Kirstin really thrived there. Since I attended with her each day, I learned about things I could do at home to help Kirstin's development. Flo explained that Kirstin, like most children, had splinter skills. She was more developed in some areas than in others. The goals were designed to help with those weaker areas. Kirstin's strengths seemed to be in verbal skills, and some of her weaker ones were in the self-help areas. One of the discussions I remember with Flo occurred when Kirstin was three. Flo was concerned that Kirstin wasn't able to put on her own socks. I couldn't understand the need for urgency there. Did she think Kirstin would go through life forever unable to fully dress herself? What excited me was the fact that Kirstin was reading the name of each child in her class from the back of the mats and telling that child which mat to sit on.

Besides working on the therapy goals, Kirstin was engaged in typical preschool activities. She did finger painting, played with age-appropriate toys, and engaged in group play with her classmates. Together, we sang all of the preschool songs, like "Old MacDonald" and "The Wheels on the Bus." Kirstin loved preschool and enjoyed all of the activities. It was obvious from the start that she was going to be her own person though. I remember one day when Kirstin was in her terrible twos (they really weren't that bad), she was supposed to be taking a nap. Flo and I were talking as quietly as we could. Suddenly, my little girl sat up and said, "Shut up, shut up. I'm the mama." Flo and I looked at each other in disbelief. Did we just hear what we thought we heard? Kirstin lay back down and finished her nap. From then on, she was known as "the Mama."

Every year there was a Christmas pageant with costumes and singing. When the preschoolers performed the *Night Before Christmas*, there was a part for a mother, but Kirstin didn't get that part. She had to settle for being a reindeer. That was her acting debut, but Kirstin would have many other opportunities to be a star.

Preschool was a comforting place. There was an atmosphere of optimism. The parents talked about kids "making it." We never exactly defined what that meant, but everyone seemed to think that Kirstin might be one who would make it. I think that if any of those parents met Kirstin today, they would say that she did. We parents were not operating under some illusion that what we were doing would somehow fix what was wrong with our kids. We all knew that wasn't possible, but just the fact that there was something we could do made all the difference. Feelings of hopefulness replaced feeling of helplessness.

Although Kirstin was progressing quite well, her teachers warned us that she would reach a plateau. There would come a point where Kirstin could progress no farther, and we should be prepared for that. Thirty-five years later, we're still waiting for her to reach that plateau. I don't think anyone working with children with Down syndrome at that time had a realistic idea about how far they could go. All of the information, studies, and actuarial tables were based on children who were institutionalized most of their lives. They probably did reach plateaus because their environment was static. Kirstin has continued to grow and develop as an adult because her environment encourages and requires her to.

There was one mother of a beautiful daughter with Down syndrome who didn't seem to be able to deal with her child's disability. She was a very young mother, which she reminded us of quite often, even though none of us was an older parent. I was twenty-six when Kirstin was born. Most of the moms were in their twenties or early thirties, but this mom was a teenager. When her daughter was two years old, the mom committed suicide, leaving a devastated husband to try to pick up the pieces. He brought his daughter to preschool and devoted himself to her progress. I remember thinking how very sad for this mom, who was going to miss seeing her daughter grow up and all the joys associated with it. Maybe the dad would remarry, and someone else would take over that role. How could she leave without seeing how her daughter's story turned out?

When Kirstin was three, her preschool started offering transportation. This was very helpful, because I had taken a teaching job at a small Christian school. All I had to do was take Kirstin to a shopping center parking lot in Chandler. She would ride in a van to Marc Center. The only problem was that she would be sitting on the lap of some adult client. Of course, that would not be legal today, but in 1978, it was acceptable transportation. We had just begun potty training with Kirstin, so I had the choice of putting her back in diapers or getting her fully trained before summer was over and the transportation would begin.

Flo gave me a book titled *Potty Training in Less Than a Day*. She said other parents had some success with it, and I decided to give it a try. The author made it quite clear that there should be no distractions, so we arranged for Craig and Michael to be gone for the day. The process was sort of a behavior modification program, with rewards for the behavior we wanted. To create as many opportunities as possible, the instructions said to give my child lots to drink. Then we practiced running to the toilet while I said, "Hurry, hurry, you have to get there fast." I was instructed to take her to various locations in the house and from there hurry to the toilet.

If Kirstin used the toilet as planned, she was given a treat, which was an M & M. She was cooperative and patient with all of this, but as the day wore on, we were both frazzled. Kirstin didn't want another M & M, and she certainly didn't want to "hurry, hurry" to the potty. I decided the real secret of potty training in less than a day was that the day was so horrible, neither mother nor child wanted to repeat it. Anyway, Kirstin was successfully potty trained, and that was the good news.

When Kirstin was four, her school was given the opportunity to enter into a joint venture with a nearby preschool so that some of the students at Marc Center could go to a regular preschool. Kirstin was chosen to be part of the first group. It was exciting to see her get what was kind of a promotion. It also served as a reality check, since it became obvious to us and to Flo that Kirstin was behind the other students. She had been a star at Marc Center. If they needed pictures for their new brochure, Kirstin would be a first choice. When the newspaper wanted to write a story about Marc Center, Kirstin was there as a shining example. Now Kirstin was not the highest in the group but the lowest.

It was at that time that I began to understand an important fact about Kirstin. Put her in a challenging situation and she will rise to meet the challenge. Before she left preschool, Kirstin knew most of the colors and recognized some numbers. Counting was difficult for her because she didn't get the one-to-one relationship. She just said the numbers in order but didn't match it to the items she was counting. Using scissors was also a challenge for her, especially when she had to cut on lines. At first, Kirstin seemed a little out of place with the other children, but eventually she fit in and made excellent social progress.

Although we had come face to face with the fact that our daughter would have limitations, it was difficult to think of her as anything but a typical child. We were doing what we could to make sure Kirstin had every chance of success in life. But we wanted her to have life experiences typical of other children her age. With her family, she went on hiking and camping trips. She traveled with us on vacations to Disneyland and even to Hawaii and Washington DC.

I knew that children her age, especially little girls, liked to take tap and ballet, so I enrolled her in a class. The teacher was kind to Kirstin, but she seemed a little uncomfortable about having her there. Kirstin paid attention and watched the other dancers. She was usually a little behind them, but there was nothing she couldn't do.

At the end of the year there was a performance. All of the little dancers wore costumes and performed for family and friends. Kirstin wore a ruffled pink costume with long pink gloves and danced to "When I Grow Up." She performed the entire dance, a little behind the others, but she watched and followed along. The dancers were crowded together, causing Kirstin to be pushed and shoved from both sides. Once she even fell forward, but she got right back up and continued. We were so proud of her.

The ballet school also had gymnastics classes, and the next year we registered Kirstin for gymnastics instead. This was a better fit, and the teacher was much more accommodating, even enthusiastic. Because she was so flexible, Kirstin was a big hit with the other gymnasts. She was the only one who could lie on her stomach and touch the bottoms of her feet to the top of her head. During the end-of-the-year performance, Kirstin was supposed to do that while the rest of the performers did a handstand, something that was difficult for Kirstin. But when the time came, she attempted the handstand instead of showing off her flexibility.

When we had a swimming pool built in our backyard, it seemed important for Kirstin to learn to swim. The Parks and Recreation Department offered lessons at our neighborhood pool. At first Kirstin did well, learning how to get safely out of the pool if she fell in. She seemed to enjoy the water and was able to dog paddle around using a kickboard. Once again, she was the poster child, posing in the pool for a news article about the swim classes.

The next year, when a new teacher took over the classes, things changed. Kirstin was afraid of the water and cried through most of the class. The teacher's method was to throw the kids into the pool and expect them to swim. This terrified Kirstin and took all of the fun out of swim lessons. Kirstin still paddled across the pool with her kickboard, but she cried the entire way. Finally, we pulled her out, not wanting to ruin swimming for her. Unfortunately, it was too late. To this day, Kirstin enjoys the pool but makes sure her feet never leave the bottom. It is sad to think that something that obviously brought Kirstin pleasure was spoiled by a teacher's "one-size-fits-all" technique. A little more patience and care could have turned swimming into a lifelong pleasure.

We continued to take Kirstin to the pediatrician who diagnosed the Down syndrome. He was supportive in most ways, but I soon learned that I had to take the initiative to make sure Kirstin received all of the medical care she needed. The first problem was with her ears. Marc Center had an audiologist check Kirstin's hearing every year, and every year the results were not good. I would take the report to her doctor, and he would look in her ears and tell me everything was okay. Finally, after the second such experience, I took her to an ear, nose, and throat specialist. He determined that Kirstin had chronic middle ear blockage and needed vent tubes to relieve the pressure.

The next issue was her eyes. One eye seemed to roll in toward her nose. I wondered how she could see properly. I asked her pediatrician about that as well, and he assured me that nothing was wrong. One day

Michael got a piece of a palm branch in his eye, and we had to take him to an ophthalmologist to have it removed. While we were there, I asked someone to take a look at Kirstin. After a quick examination, the doctor advised us to make an appointment. The diagnosis was strabismus, also called wall eye, and because of it, Kirstin was seeing double. I remember the ophthalmologist asking Kirstin to look at me and tell her how many moms she saw. Kirstin said, "Two." For the first four years of her life, she had two moms. Imagine that.

Kirstin was fitted for glasses. They were bifocals with very thick lenses. The line in the bifocals was there to break up her vision and allow both eyes to work together. Her vision improved so much that Kirstin insisted on having her glasses right by her bed, so she could put them on before getting up. There has never been an issue with Kirstin wearing her glasses. Even when they rub a sore behind her ear, she won't leave them off.

The ophthalmologist asked me the name of Kirstin's doctor. When I told her, she said that he was usually very good at spotting this problem. She couldn't imagine how he missed it. I couldn't imagine that either, since I had pointed it out to him on many occasions. Maybe he wanted to spare us the expense of getting Kirstin's hearing and vision fixed. I never asked him why. All I knew was that Kirstin needed the best tools available to access her environment. That meant two good ears and two good eyes. Getting those things taken care of was certainly money well spent.

Marc Center was more than just a preschool. It provided for the needs of special people of all ages. There was a day program for school-aged children who were considered trainable mentally disabled. In addition, adults received services from Marc Center that included independent living skills and vocational training.

In 1975 Congress passed Public Law 94-142 (Education of All Handicapped Children Act). Today it is known as IDEA (Individuals with Disabilities Education Act). It requires school districts to provide a free, appropriate public education to all children no matter what the disability. Over the years it has been redefined and today carries so much clout that it sends school districts into a tizzy trying to comply. In 1975 the concept was new, but school districts had to figure out a way to include these students in their schools or face losing federal funds. What that meant at Marc Center was that they no longer needed a program for school-age children. Starting in the fall of 1976, all of their students would be going to public school.

Since we came on the scene the year 94-142 went into effect, we never saw what the school program was like at Marc Center. But we did have a great deal of involvement in the adult program. Our experiences at Marc Center opened up a whole new world to us. It was a world of shocking truths and amazing changes. We were there to witness them all.

At that time, the Arizona legislature was holding hearings about what should be done with a residential facility in Coolidge, Arizona. It was home to hundreds of people with mental retardation who had been institutionalized there, some of them since birth. Housed in a clinical setting, most residents had no hope of ever leaving. Families had been encouraged to place their children there and many of those children spent their entire lives institutionalized. Now those people who had been isolated from society were asking for a chance to live in a home like everyone else. Craig and I attended some of the hearings. We sat in awe of those residents from the institution who now stood before the legislative committee and pleaded their case. I can't imagine how I would feel having to face such a panel, but these people were articulate and sure of what they were asking. I thought of other minority groups who had to fight for equal rights. Like Martin Luther King Jr., they were talking about their dreams for a brighter future. I thought of Chief Seattle, asking for fair treatment for his people, or Cesar Chavez and the California grape growers, fighting for fair working conditions. They did not expect someone else to speak for them but stood up for themselves just like any other group of people battling injustice. What they wanted is what was spoken of in the Bill of Rights . . . life, liberty, and the pursuit of happiness. They wanted to be able to live as independently as possible in the community with the rest of us. It seemed like a simple truth to me; they should have that right.

Fortunately, the Arizona legislature saw it that way as well. As a result of these hearings, most of the Coolidge facility was closed, and all but the most severe residents were placed in group homes in communities throughout Arizona. Of course there were some difficulties with neighbors who had no knowledge of people with cognitive challenges. Some were convinced that their new neighbors were oversexed and unable to control themselves. But little by little, the former residents of the Coolidge facility won their rights and adjusted to their new lives.

We met a man who had lived in an institution for thirty years and was now learning to balance his own checkbook. Like many others, he was benefiting from participation in the adult program at Marc Center. Their levels of abilities varied, and so did their needs, but now they had a chance to live as independently as they were capable of. It was an amazing experience, and we felt so fortunate to be a part of it.

Craig served on the board of directors of Marc Center for many years and was serving as the president when they hired Phil Barnum to run their sheltered workshop. Phil was a retired design engineer for Boeing. He was a master at creating jigs that enabled the workers with cognitive challenges to produce products for several local manufacturers at a competitive rate. The sheltered workshop was a business that made money.

Today, Marc Center provides a variety of programs to meet the needs of people with developmental disabilities. Families who go to them for assistance are able to choose what best meets their needs in order to prepare their children for whatever level of independence they can reach. This might be living at home with their families, moving into a group home, living semi-independently, or living totally on their own. Employment opportunities vary from the sheltered workshop to full competitive employment. For those unable to work, day programs fill their lives with meaningful activities. The world of the specially challenged has changed a great deal since 1975, when Kirstin and special education were born.

Parents today are supported by government agencies. In Arizona it is called the Division of Developmental Disabilities (DDD). Families are assigned a support coordinator, who determines their needs. Parents are given a budget and are able to shop for services with various providers. In this way, they have input into who will be working with their child and what that person will be doing. Competition among providers also benefits the families as consumers. Services might include habilitation, respite care, and therapies such as speech, occupational, and physical. Depending on the age of the child, habilitation could involve working on daily living skills, community access, shopping, or independent living. Respite care provides a break for the family and a chance to get away for a day or even for a vacation. Caring for a special needs child with multiple disabilities is a full-time job, and caregivers benefit greatly from getting a breather. As children get older, DDD stays on board to help with vocational planning and decisions about where the person will live as an adult. Continuing support is available for adults who want to become fully independent but need help reaching that goal.

Today, there is only one intermediate care facility in Arizona. It houses about one hundred residents whose needs are so severe that they are unable to survive outside a clinical setting. In the past five years, no new patients have been added to that facility. The goal of the DDD is to keep those with intellectual challenges in their homes if at all possible. In fact, Arizona ranks number one in the country in that regard. In addition to living at home, supported living arrangements and group homes are also very good options. Ultimately, the choice comes down to the person with the special needs, and that is as it should be.

We didn't realize it at the time, but we had entered a world that would become a huge part of our lives. Craig's service on the board at Marc Center and my participation at the preschool left us wanting to become even more involved. I eventually became a special education teacher. We started the Bradshaw Mountain Special Olympics group with full family involvement and continued to assist with Special Olympics until Kirstin decided to give it up. Craig was the sponsor of Prescott Oasis, a self-advocacy group for adults with developmental disabilities. We meet our special needs friends everywhere we go and enjoy spending time with them. They will always be important people in our lives. In fact, I couldn't imagine life without them. It really is a wonderful world.

> ## KIRSTIN'S SIDE OF THE STORY
>
> *I do think about people with disabilities every day. Everybody should be treated nicely by other people. We all need to have respect for each other every day. Some of my friends are in wheelchairs. Some are blind. They need more help than I do. They have nice caregivers who take them lots of places. I help them if I can. One way I help them is by being their friend.*

Chapter Three

ఐఁ

Getting Schooled

A graduation was held for all of the students at Marc Center who would be enrolled in kindergarten in the fall. Kirstin attended, dressed in a pink and white checked dress with a white pinafore, and she looked adorable. While she was going to the regular preschool, Kirstin had been away from most of the other students at Marc Center. Now that she was reunited with them, she didn't seem to fit in. For most of the graduation ceremony, Kirstin remained quiet and aloof, not her usual gregarious self. It seemed that my five-year-old daughter was a snob. By the end of the celebration, though, she became her old self again and joined in with everyone else. Still, I couldn't help but wonder if this was a sign of things to come.

Thinking ahead to Kirstin's first year in public school, Flo suggested that we begin looking at what Chandler School District had to offer. I contacted the special services director and was told about the programs that were available. Then Flo and I visited them together. The first program we looked at was for students who were considered *trainable*. I didn't like the sound of that. What were they going to train her to do? I thought schools were supposed to educate students. Nevertheless, I tried to go there with an open mind.

The trainable program was housed in a very small, enclosed room in an elementary school. At the time we visited, there was only one student in the room, along with the teacher. Apparently there were three other students, who were at recess with the aide. The student who remained in the room had not done his work and, therefore, could not go out to recess. I guessed that he was about nine years old or a little older by his size. He was overweight and would have benefited greatly from going outside for exercise. There were a few worksheets on his desk, but he was not engaged in doing them during the time we were there. The room was very plain and uninteresting, and the teacher seemed like a real taskmaster. Flo and I agreed that this would not be a place we would ever consider for Kirstin.

At another school, there was a program for students considered to be *educable*. That sounded better, and it was. Students there were working on pre-reading academic skills, similar to what Kirstin had been engaged in during preschool. It was a class for kindergarten through third grade. Students advanced from there to another class once they reached fourth grade. We visited the middle-grade class as well. The teacher there was very enthusiastic, and her students seemed to be enjoying what they were involved with. It was a big class with lots of activities going on. I was excited about the prospect of Kirstin eventually being in that class.

After visiting all of the special education classes, Flo and I agreed that Kirstin had the same needs as any other student starting kindergarten. She had to make the transition from preschool to public school. She needed to gain some basic skills, like counting and learning the alphabet. Finally, she needed to learn how to get along with the teachers and the other students. She could accomplish all of that in a kindergarten class, and the following year she would be ready to go into the class for educable students.

Since the special education classes Kirstin would go into were at Frye School, we wanted her to attend kindergarten at Frye, even though it was not our neighborhood school. In that way, Kirstin would not have to make an adjustment to a new school after kindergarten. The whole plan made perfect sense to us but was a little frightening for the administration at Frye School. At the time mainstreaming meant spending a small part of the school day in a regular class, assisted by an aide. What we were asking for was full inclusion, and I'm not sure public education in Chandler was ready for that.

At the placement meeting, we faced off across the table from the principal, the special education director, the kindergarten teacher, and the special education teacher. On our side were my husband, myself, Flo Smith, the preschool director, and Kirstin's DDD coordinator. We had them outnumbered. By the end of the meeting, all agreed that Kirstin would be placed in the kindergarten class. We asked for the same services she was receiving at the Marc Center. These included speech therapy, occupational therapy, and physical therapy. At the time, Chandler was only providing speech therapy. As a result of that meeting, DDD would be providing the other two services not only for Kirstin but for other students as well.

All things considered, we thought the meeting was a big success. That was at least until we asked about transportation. Kirstin would not be attending her neighborhood school and would need to be bused. The view of the school district was that since Kirstin was to be in a regular kindergarten, she did not qualify for special transportation. Our DDD coordinator pointed out the error in their thinking. The law was on our side, and so every day, a big yellow bus stopped at our house for one tiny passenger.

Now that Kirstin was in kindergarten, her Individual Program Plan was replaced by an Individual Education Plan (IEP). Just like the IPP, the IEP included a list of goals for the coming year and the services that would be provided by the school district. As parents, we were invited to participate in planning the IEP. Having Kirstin's preschool teacher at the meeting helped assure a smooth transition.

Kirstin's first year in public school was a success in some ways but difficult in other ways. As much as we thought Kirstin was prepared for school, she was still behind the other children, and her progress was less than we had hoped. She did not participate in group activities such as singing or art. On the playground, little boys fed her sand. She wandered away and had to be supervised at all times. In spite the problems, testing at the end of the school year did reveal progress. When she entered kindergarten, she could recognize six out of eight colors, one out of ten numbers, and could not count at all. By the end of kindergarten, she could identify eight out of eight colors, four out of four shapes, nine out of ten numbers, twenty-two out of twenty-six letters, count to five, and print her name. Her scores put her in the fourteenth percentile, but taking into account where she was when she began, that was amazing progress.

We also found out that Kirstin was learning to stand up for herself. One day I received a phone call from a somewhat frustrated principal, who told me that Kirstin had come to his office on her own. She told him that someone on the playground had pulled down her pants. The principal wasn't sure what to do, because Kirstin, hands on hips, kept insisting, "The pink girl did it." Unable to identify the "pink girl," he said there wasn't much he could do except ask the playground aides to keep an eye out. We were satisfied with that and also relieved to see that Kirstin was learning to handle her own problems.

It is doubtful that the "pink girl" was someone in Kirstin's class. If that had been the case, Kirstin would have known her name. At the end of the kindergarten year, there was a promotion celebration in her classroom. The teacher talked about each student and his or her special abilities. Kirstin, we found out, was the only student in the class who knew everybody's name. While her social skills might be lagging, she certainly was paying attention, and she could remember things that were important to her.

Kirstin started first grade in Mrs. Blanton's self-contained class. The trainable class was never mentioned as a possible placement, much to our relief. As with kindergarten, there were difficulties. In her progress reports, Mrs. Blanton wrote things like, "Unable to function" ... "needs an aide" ... "constant supervision" ... "unable to understand" ... "refuses to work." In spite of all the negatives, Kirstin still managed to master twelve out of the sixteen goals on her IEP. She was beginning to read sight words and learn phonics. She could add using manipulatives and count to ten. Kirstin was interacting better with her classmates.

Pronouncing her name had always been difficult for Kirstin. No matter how hard she tried, it came out "Dursen." When she began learning letters and sounds, she knew this was wrong. "Dursen has a k," she would say. To help her out, we gave her the nickname, "Kiki." She liked that, and so until she could pronounce her name correctly, we called her Kiki. Sometimes I even called her Kiki Sue. Once in a while I still call her that.

While Kirstin was receiving her free, appropriate, public education, we as parents were getting schooled as well. We were beginning to understand our role in the education process and the importance of our involvement in the decisions that were being made on Kirstin's behalf. We were her advocates, and it was our responsibility to make sure she received the best educational opportunities available. When Kirstin was in preschool, we took an active role in the planning and even the execution of her IPP. It was not in our nature to take a backseat just because she was now in public school. Looking back, I can see that we didn't always handle each situation in the best possible way, but we never relinquished our rights as parents to participate in the educational planning for our daughter. While we never demanded something the district was unable to provide, we did make sure they always provided a challenging and motivating program that enabled Kirstin to succeed to the highest level of her ability.

Kirstin finished second grade in Mrs. Blanton's class. She continued to show progress but was not yet reading well. Toward the end of that school year, the Chandler district was making plans to move the special education classes out of Frye School. The possibility of such a change brought a crowd of angry parents to the school board meetings. When the school bond was passed to build Frye Elementary, the district asked for the new school partly as a facility for special education. Now the plan was to move the special education classes to an obscure corner of an older campus, making mainstreaming almost impossible. The facilities at Frye were modern and located right in the hub of the school. Sending special education to the "south forty" seemed like stepping back into the dark ages of special education. We attended some of the school board hearings, but since we were already planning to move north, we never quite heard how things turned out. Today, Chandler has an outstanding special education program that serves students with all types of disabilities. Like all districts at the time, they were experiencing growing pains.

Our move to Prescott Valley in the summer of 1983 meant that Kirstin would be enrolled in a new school. Humboldt Unified School District was very small but growing. That year they were adding a self-contained program at Lake Valley Elementary and hired as their first teacher Dorothy Mobley. I had the opportunity to meet her ahead of time, because she attended our church. Dorothy, like us, had just moved to Prescott Valley, and like me, she was applying for her first special education position. She was very enthusiastic and had high expectations for her students. As a student in her class, Kirstin learned to read, spell, add, and subtract. She could count money, and tell time. Mrs. Mobley wrote: "Kirstin has shown much improvement in all areas. Her socialization skills and attitudes are very good. She is self-confident and answers each request to demonstrate a new skill by saying 'I'll try.' She is not only a delight to have in class, but a lot of fun."

Kirstin made great progress at Lake Valley Elementary. She loved school, and she loved her teacher. After two years, Mrs. Mobley's class became too large, and another teacher was hired to teach the more capable students. Kirstin remained in Mrs. Mobley's class until I found out about the higher-level class. Immediately, I went to work getting Kirstin moved to that class. Knowing how she strived to reach whatever standard is set for her, I knew she needed to be challenged. And so she was, and so she met the challenges. Her reading and writing skills continued to improve. Math was another story. Kirstin struggled with math and at one point announced to me that she did not need to learn math because she had a calculator. She was exited from occupational therapy, because she no longer needed it. She continued to receive speech therapy.

By the time Kirstin was ready for middle school, we had moved to Chino Valley, an even smaller community with a smaller school district.

The special education director there convinced us to keep Kirstin at their elementary school, because the district did not yet have enough students for a program at the middle school. Knowing how important social development was to Kirstin, we agreed that placement at the elementary school was best for the time being.

Kirstin's teachers at Del Rio School were encouraging and supportive. Although she was in a self-contained class, she was able to spend time each day with her nondisabled peers. Patty La Fleur was Kirstin's first teacher at Del Rio. She was so excited about having Kirstin in her class. Mrs. La Fleur told me that she looked at her new class and fell instantly in love with them. I do know what she was talking about, because I've had the same feeling. But I've never heard another teacher express that feeling out loud. Mrs. La Fleur has a great love for reading, and this she passed on to Kirstin. By that time, Kirstin's reading skills were advanced enough so that she could read chapter books. Kirstin immediately fell in love with *The Baby-Sitter's Club* by Ann Martin.

The occupational therapist at Del Rio had a wonderful program, so Kirstin once again received occupational therapy. Instead of working on skills in isolation, she took her students out into the community. With other students, Kirstin went to the bank, the gym, or various other businesses in town. Kirstin enjoyed these activities, and it gave her self-confidence and skills to manage her environment.

A psychological test given when Kirstin was twelve indicated some real improvement. The report read in part: "It was noted during the last complete assessment that Kirstin exhibited many self-distracting behaviors indicative of a short attention and impulsivity. During the current assessment Kirstin's attention to task was excellent. She willingly accompanied the examiner to the testing room, and rapport was easily established. Kirstin demonstrated an adequate focus and concentration in all presented activities. She approached all tasks with cooperation and enthusiasm." It was obvious Kirstin hadn't hit any plateaus, at least not yet.

Of course there were still problems. Kirstin had her own little world, and sometimes it interfered with the real world. One day when I picked up our mail at the post office, I was surprised to find a letter from Kirstin's teacher. She was obviously distressed about a note Kirstin had written to her. In the note, Kirstin accused the playground aide of being a witch and casting evil spells on the students. My first reaction was to laugh, but Kirstin was with me, so I had to keep a straight face. We talked about why it was not appropriate, and Kirstin promised not to do it again.

Finally, after being asked to hold Kirstin back in elementary school year after year for four years, we insisted that she be allowed to go to middle school. Otherwise, it was unlikely that she would be able to finish high school by age twenty-two, the limit for public education in our state. Even after all the waiting, Kirstin was still the only extended resource student at Heritage Middle School. This presented some problems, because she didn't quite fit in anywhere. For most of Kirstin's day, four periods, she was in the resource room.

There were some attempts at mainstreaming. For example, Kirstin was in a regular social studies class. When I say she was "in" the class, I mean that she sat in the classroom. During that time, Kirstin was with an aide, working from a lower-level text. This continued until the teacher had problems with some of the boys in the class. Although the problems had nothing to do with Kirstin, part of the solution was to move her somewhere else. That never really made sense to me, but hopefully it did to someone. It seemed that Kirstin was being punished for someone else's bad behavior. At least she was still in regular art and music classes.

The program at the middle school also included functional life skills classes. Kirstin had difficulty understanding many of the life skills concepts but enjoyed the hands-on activities, such as cooking, and the field trips. She learned about managing time and money, reading maps and signs, and using the phone book and the library.

Behavior continued to be a problem, and I was called to her school many times to discuss it. Kirstin had trouble staying on task and would spend her time reading *The Baby-Sitter's Club* instead of what she was supposed to be doing. Some of Kirstin's old behaviors resurfaced, such as pulling her coat over her head and refusing to come into the classroom.

I suspect that the problems were partly due to the fact that Kirstin was isolated a good part of the day, and she knew she didn't quite fit in. One solution suggested by the special education director was to tuition Kirstin to my school district. I didn't take them up on their offer, although I'm not really sure why. Perhaps I was thinking that if Kirstin was going to make it in the world, she had to learn to make the best of every situation.

Speech continued to be an area where progress was slow. Kirstin still talked too fast and put her head down when she spoke. Articulation was her biggest problem, and the speech therapist seemed to think that getting her teeth straightened would be a great help. We had already taken her to the orthodontist who put braces on Michael's teeth. He didn't do much for Kirstin at first, except take X-rays, and then we waited. Finally, after two years of waiting and listening to the speech therapist remind us that something needed to be done, the orthodontist put in a palate spreader. This was intended to make more room in her mouth. Once that was accomplished, the next logical step should have been braces, but once again he delayed. It eventually became obvious to us that he was never going to really help her.

Our dentist recommended another orthodontist, who had worked with patients with a cleft palate. He would provide the help Kirstin needed, though a little bit late; Kirstin would wear braces for most of high school. But he really accomplished a miracle. Many of Kirstin's baby teeth didn't have permanent teeth under them. This was not a big problem, because her mouth was too small for the normal number of teeth. There was one tooth, however, that the orthodontist really needed to save in order to have enough teeth for what he had planned. Unfortunately, it was growing downward, toward her jaw. Our orthodontist's solution was to attach a jeweler's chain to the tooth in an effort to pull it up. The chain came loose after a while and had to be reattached. Eventually the tooth was in place, and it was time for braces. Our orthodontist thought Kirstin's palate could be spread even more, but there was some urgency there. This had to be done by age eighteen, or it might be too late.

Kirstin was very responsible with her braces and did everything she was asked to do. She wore her rubber bands and later, her retainer, which meant that the end result was very good. In her lifetime, Kirstin has only had one very small cavity, which I think is amazing in itself. When her braces were removed, she had beautiful, straight teeth. Her speech did improve considerably, and her tongue no longer protruded.

Kirstin was finishing eighth grade, and it was nearly time for graduation. The eighth-graders were going on a field trip, but because Kirstin was shuffled around so much, she didn't get a permission slip. No one realized that until the day of the field trip, so Kirstin wasn't allowed to go. Knowing that she was the only eighth-grader left on campus, she ditched her classes and hid out. She was caught, of course, and she was assigned a day of in-school suspension (ISS) as punishment.

It would have been easy to intercede for her. After all, her teacher had failed to give her a permission slip. But we decided to let Kirstin serve her punishment and spend the day in ISS. She needed to face the consequences of the choices she made, regardless of the circumstances. This was an opportunity for Kirstin to grow as a responsible person, and that was our major concern.

After Kirstin was out of high school, we were shopping at K-mart one day. Kirstin was in line in front of me, and my cart was between us. She was handling her own transactions, conversing with the clerk, and paying with her debit card. The woman behind me, recognizing that Kirstin and I were together, made the comment, "She does very well, doesn't she?"

I responded, "Yes, Kirstin is very independent." The other shopper was surprised to hear me call her Kirstin. "That's Kirstin?" she said. "I used to be her speech therapist when she was in middle school. You've done very well with her."

The fact is Kirstin's speech therapist also played a role in helping her become an independent young lady. Often teachers and therapists, especially at the elementary level, never get to see the end result of their hard work. We are all the sum of our experiences, and school plays a big part in shaping who we will become. While not every aspect of Kirstin's elementary and middle-school experience was what we might have hoped, in the long run, I can say it was more than adequate to prepare Kirstin for what would come next... high school and beyond.

> ## KIRSTIN'S SIDE OF THE STORY
>
> *I remember I had a friend in school named Tiffany Porter. She went to Lake Valley and to Del Rio. I liked all my teachers but sometimes I gave them a hard time. I was teased by some kids at Del Rio.*
>
> *My favorite teacher in middle school was Mrs. Henry. She was gorgeous, with beautiful black hair. She dressed very nicely. I wrote letters to her, and she laughed at them. Connie Smith teased me because I like New Kids on the Block. After I told her sister, she stopped teasing me.*

Chapter Four
ಏಐ
Living with Bratinella

This chapter had to be written lest you get the idea that Kirstin was a perfect child and we were the luckiest parents on the planet. Books and chapters in books have been written about the behaviors of children with Down syndrome. I always remind myself of what the doctor told me: "Everything your read is true, but it won't necessarily be true for your child." That has proved to be excellent advice. I'm sure Kirstin would like to skip this chapter, and she'll have some very interesting things to say at the end, but it still has to be written. There were some very good reasons we gave her the nickname "Bratinella."

When Kirstin was about four years old, she started doing something that left us wondering what we, as parents, were in for. Every time we dined at a restaurant, Kirstin would wait until we had all finished eating before she began her meal. At first, we wouldn't notice; everyone was talking and not really paying attention to Kirstin. Later we tried to encourage her to eat, but because she was stubborn or for reasons of her own, she wouldn't eat. The rest of us felt like we were being held hostage by a small child, as Kirstin slowly consumed her meal with all of us watching. It was pretty obvious what Kirstin was getting out of it. She was calling the shots and controlling her entire family. Now she had our undivided attention.

Because she only weighed about twenty-two pounds, we were reluctant to have her go without eating. That put us in the difficult situation of learning to live with Kirstin's stubbornness, force-feeding her, or taking doggy bags so she could eat in the car. Afraid that this could become a pattern, I decided something had to be done. The next time we were dining out, Kirstin sat as we all ate our dinners. We tried not to notice and just carried on a normal conversation. When we were all finished, true to form, Kirstin began slowly eating. I stood up and announced, "Well, we need to get going."

To this, Kirstin responded, "I'm not done."

"Too bad," I said. "You should have eaten while you had the chance." Then we took her by the hand and left the restaurant, leaving her uneaten meal behind. To our relief, we only had to do that once. The next time we were dining out, Kirstin ate her dinner with the rest of us.

We learned a few things from that experience. First of all, we learned how easily we could be manipulated by this tiny child. But we also learned that she could figure things out for herself. If we remained consistent in our expectations, Kirstin would be able to make good choices, and life would be better for all of us.

Other parents of children with Down syndrome have told me how their child talks to him—or herself. This seems to be a common trend. In Kirstin's case, she perfected it to an art form. Not only did she have an imaginary friend to talk to, she had an entire family she called "the group." At one time, I believe there were seven members of her group. She carried on conversations with them, shared her food with them, and took them everywhere she went. Going in her bedroom, she would hold the door open until everyone was in. Then, through the closed door, we would hear lots of talking from many different voices. She never gave us much information about who these friends were. I did get a few names: Harry, Little Terry, and Big Terry. I was somewhat concerned about Harry when I learned that he had horns. But Kirstin assured me he was a good guy.

In a way, it seemed convenient that Kirstin always had friends. Her brother, Michael, is four years older chronologically, but if you consider maturity, there was an even greater age difference. Besides, being a boy, he had totally different interests from Kirstin. She was always busy with her own activities, happy with what she was doing, and never really alone because she had her group. It did cause her problems at school, when she would get so busy with her imaginary friends that she forgot to pay attention. More than once her teachers sent reports about Kirstin doing her own thing instead of what she was supposed to be doing. Eventually, she would do her work but in her own good time. One report read, "Kirstin is eager to please for most of her work. Sometimes she still continues to use her time for her 'club' activities. I insist she do her work. She gets mad and then does what I ask and usually does it well!"

Kirstin was approaching her twelfth birthday, and it seemed like a good idea for her to stop having imaginary friends. She would be going to middle school, and the kids might make fun of her. Besides, she needed to face reality. After a serious discussion about the group, Kirstin agreed that by her twelfth birthday, they would be gone. And it seemed that she was true to her word.

It was a few months after Kirstin turned twelve that we were shopping in a fabric store. Kirstin was looking at the racks of fabric and talking incessantly to someone who wasn't really there. I reminded her that she promised her group would go away.

"They did," she told me, "but they're here shopping with their mom."

Today, in private places like the bathroom, Kirstin can be overheard talking to someone, and I've watched her at work, whispering under her breath. She claims to have no memory of her imaginary friends, but I guess we'll never know. Someone pointed out to me that with Kirstin's June birthday, she is a Gemini, the twin. Maybe that explains it, but I don't know too much about that.

Kirstin's most annoying habit was that of disappearing. Houdini himself could have taken lessons from her. And, of course, she would choose the time and place to vanish when it was most disruptive to our plans. When we lived in Chandler and Kirstin was about five years old, Fiesta Mall was being built in Mesa. Though the mall was under construction, the Sears store was up and running. We liked to shop at Sears, sometimes for things we needed but other times just to look around. Kirstin's first disappearing act occurred when she decided to go to the restroom on her own. It was a little scary for a few minutes, but we found her and all was well.

On later trips to Sears, it became routine for Kirstin to wander off and for us to spend a few minutes searching for her. We were never too concerned, because she didn't get that far away, and it was almost like a game to go hunting for her. That was until one day we were frightened out of our skins. Kirstin was missing as usual, and we were looking for her as always, but we were unaware that the entire Fiesta Mall had been completed. After scouring the Sears store for about fifteen minutes, we walked to the door that exited into the mall. There before us lay a huge cavernous mall that, for all we knew, had swallowed up our tiny child. The feeling of helplessness was overwhelming.

We stood for a few minutes in shock, unsure what to do, until suddenly a security guard came down the steps from the second floor, holding Kirstin's hand. She had a cookie in the other hand and seemed quite pleased with herself. The security guard asked us several questions to make sure we were her parents and looked at us as if questioning what kind of parents would let such a small child wander around on her own. That certainly added to the guilt we were feeling.

The mall adventure was not my worst experience with Kirstin's vanishing acts. That happened later the same year, at Christmastime, when everybody is hustling and bustling along and trying to get everything done. Craig was the president of the Arizona Jaycees, and I was given the task of sending out over a hundred Christmas cards. I had the cards addressed but waited until I bought the stamps at the post office to put on the postage. As I applied stamp after stamp to the envelopes, Kirstin played on the steps nearby. Engrossed in what I was doing, I didn't notice she had left. I looked up and suddenly realized that Kirstin was no longer on the steps. She wasn't anywhere in the post office. I asked a worker to check in the back, and she wasn't there either. That was when I called the police.

Panic was setting in, but I went outside and walked around the entire building. Then I stopped people coming through the drive-thru to ask if they had seen her. Busy as everyone was, the work at the post office came to a grinding halt, while workers and customers helped. People coming through the drive-thru offered to drive around the neighborhood to look for her. The generosity of people was overwhelming, but my daughter was nowhere.

After what seemed like hours, a patrol car drove up. When the officer got out of his car, he opened the back door, and I saw her. She was fine, not the least bit shook up until her mom grabbed her and held on for dear life. Then the story came out. A friend who was eating in Bob's Big Boy recognized Kirstin and stopped her. As I was calling the police to report Kirstin missing, she was calling the police to report her found. With her head down and walking as if she knew where she was going, Kirstin had apparently marched down the main street in Chandler for almost a mile.

I wish I could say that was the end of Kirstin's adventures, but unfortunately, she continued to frighten her family for many years to come. She loved the mirrors in dressing rooms, and that was usually where we found her. Of course she would be talking to her imaginary friends quite loudly, and so we knew where she was. We thought about getting one of those leashes you see parents using sometimes, but that just didn't seem right. Kirstin wasn't trying to make our lives a nightmare; she just was off in her own little world. Over time, she came to like the real world more and grew out of her need to wander away.

On a few occasions, Kirstin was able to take advantage of some electric conveyance to aid in her escape. Her brother, Michael, talks about a time when Kirstin took a daring ride on an escalator at the mall. Instead of stepping on the stairs as they appeared, Kirstin grabbed hold of the outside of the handrail. Before we knew what was happening, she was carried upward, clinging to the side of the elevator like a monkey. As Michael describes it, "She went up the wall." Actually, she was traveling in the space between the wall and the escalator. Responding quickly, Craig ran up the escalator and snatched her from a potentially tragic end to her ride.

It was just Kirstin and I together on another escalator adventure. Kirstin was a preschooler, and the two of us were shopping in a large department store. I was carrying two huge bags filled with purchases and let go of Kirstin's hand briefly to adjust them. In the short span of a few seconds, Kirstin took the opportunity to hop on the escalator. With little time to react, I jumped on after her. As I bent down to scoop Kirstin up, the strap on my handbag fell off my shoulder and became entangled in my feet. There was no way to free myself without the risk of dropping my packages, Kirstin, or both. As we rode to the top of the escalator, I contemplated how I was going to extricate myself from this mess. At the same time, I knew there was a distinct possibility that we would both plummet to a painful death. When we reached the top, I was somehow able to get us off the escalator. I waited until I stopped shaking before attempting the trip back down.

On another occasion, it was an elevator that carried Kirstin away, this time purely by accident. We were on a vacation to New Orleans, where we had reservations at a Holiday Inn just off Bourbon Street. We parked our car in the parking garage. Craig and I were busy getting the luggage out of the car when Kirstin, now about fourteen, spotted the elevator. She pushed the button, and when the door opened, not realizing we weren't ready yet, got into the elevator. Without her knowing this could happen, the doors closed on her and she was whisked away. In my mind, this elevator was something like the Wonkavator from *Charlie and the Chocolate Factory,* the one that could go upways and downways and sideways and crossways. Although Kirstin entered the elevator in the parking garage, she ended up in the hotel. Fortunately, there were cameras on the elevators, and after showing us a few children we didn't recognize, security was able to locate Kirstin, who was on her way down from the top floor. (It's a good thing there wasn't an up and out button like the one in the Wonkavator.) After what seemed like an eternity, the elevator door opened, and Kirstin walked out, happy to see us.

Of course, Kirstin picked up some bad habits from her brother. As he was our firstborn, we were just learning to be parents and sometimes overreacted. Michael was a talkative, friendly child who never met a stranger. Wherever we were, it seemed that he would meet someone—a nicely dressed working person or a ragged-looking street person, he made no distinction. He would immediately strike up a conversation with the stranger, and in the course of speaking to him, Michael would always invite him to our home. He would ask, "Do you know where we live?" To which the person would naturally reply, "No, I don't." Then Michael would tell him to, "Just follow us home." Fortunately for us, no one ever took Michael up on the offer.

When Kirstin came along, she picked up his knack for meeting strangers and talking to everyone she met. Fortunately, she was harder to understand and didn't think about inviting people to our home. But she did develop another of her brother's bad habits. When they were young children, we owned a Circle K convenience store franchise. Quite often, we would stop at the store on our way somewhere, because Craig had something he needed to do or had to leave instructions with a worker. Of course, there is nothing a child likes better than to have a parent with a candy store. So every time we stopped in, Michael and Kirstin wanted candy or soda or something. Afraid this would become a routine, we told them they could not ask for anything. Michael, being the resourceful boy that he was, would go outside and walk around the store, checking in the weeds of the vacant lot next door. Pretty soon he would come back in with enough returnable pop bottles to get money for whatever he wanted. Kirstin, as you can well understand, was not allowed outside the store. But she developed her own method of getting what she wanted. She panhandled. It took us a while to figure out what was going on, but she was asking customers to buy her what she wanted. We had to tell her she couldn't do that anymore, but we also had to educate our customers, who were softies when it came to the cute little beggar.

As all brothers do, Michael enjoyed teasing his little sister. Sometimes this consisted of sitting on her bed when she told him to get out of her room. Other times he would dress up in his Jason mask and scare her. Kirstin would shriek in fear and come running to us, faking some tears. Secretly, I think she enjoyed the game and was just playing her part. But she did seem to get a little too much pleasure out of telling on her brother.

Hands down, our scariest moments as the parents of Bratinella happened shortly after our move to Chino Valley. Michael, who was now in high school, was at home with Kirstin. He went out riding his ATV while she was watching television. For some reason only known to her—maybe she was bored—she started striking matches and throwing them into a wastebasket. When that caught on fire, she moved on to the kitchen trash can. Pretty soon, it was ablaze as well. Knowing what to do, Kirstin called 911 to report the fires. The operator asked for her address, but since we hadn't lived there long, she didn't know it. "I'll have to get my library card," she told the operator before laying down the phone and going to her bedroom. Unable to find her library card, she returned to the phone and was told to go to a neighbor's house and have them call 911. Now Kirstin needed her shoes, which were also misplaced. When no other solution presented itself, Kirstin sat down and continued watching television. That was when her brother came inside. He immediately put out the fires. One had burned through the carpet, and he went down stairs to make sure it wasn't burning through the floor.

By the time we came home, the fires were out. Shaking and not sure what to do, I ordered Kirstin to clean the wall that was black. For two hours, I made her scrub the wall. "I'm too tired," she complained. But I insisted there was more black to wash off. Later, after I had calmed down, we talked about what could have been the consequences if Michael hadn't acted so quickly. She could have died in the fire, along with our pets. Kirstin was able to grasp the seriousness of what she had done, and the incident was never repeated. After a short while, we relaxed and were able to trust her at home alone once again.

As Kirstin grew out of her Bratinella stage, we gave her a new nickname. We started calling her "Doctor Kirstin." This was because she decided that it was her role in our family to arbitrate any disagreement. Kirstin would sit down between the two people arguing and say, "Okay, tell your side." This, of course, made the family members having the argument even madder, but now they were mad at Kirstin. It was especially frustrating for Michael, who was a teenager and not too likely to take advice from his little sister. Still, she did manage to end the arguing. While we didn't really let her settle our disputes, she did distract us from whatever we were arguing about. We would say, "All right, Doctor Kirstin, we don't need any counseling."

Really, we couldn't help laughing when Doctor Kirstin was "in." She had such a way of making our arguments seem superfluous and uniting us as a family. I remember one time Kirstin and I were in the car. I was angry with Craig for some reason, and I was going on and on about it. Kirstin was quiet for a while and then I heard, "God wants you to love your husband." How could I possibly stay mad at him after that?

Most parents of children with Down syndrome will talk about stubbornness, but it is not the kind of stubbornness other parents encounter. Children with Down syndrome seem to like their routines. In Kirstin's case, and I've had other parents tell me the same thing, it is her own routine. We never gave her a bedtime; we didn't have to. Kirstin always determined her own bedtime and went to bed on her own. The time she chose was usually some very specific time, like 9:36. We probably would have set her bedtime at 10:00, but there was no need for that when Kirstin went to bed every night at 9:36 on the dot. This sounds wonderful until something interferes with that bedtime. Over the years, Kirstin has become more flexible, and as an adult, she adjusts to the world. But as a child, it was difficult for her to make changes in her routine.

Kirstin likes order in her world, and so her CDs are in alphabetical order, as are her movies. When she gets a new one, she finds where it belongs in the order and then moves all of the ones after that. Sometimes this takes a long time, but I think she actually enjoys the process. She has certain tasks that she does each day, like Monday is laundry day. She will rearrange her schedule when something special is going to be happening, but she likes to know ahead of time, so she can get used to the idea. She has certain foods that she eats on certain days, and there is a problem if she runs out of something that she needs that day.

Kirstin is a clock watcher, and she has owned a calendar every year since she was eight. In October she starts looking for one for the next year. When she lived at home, she made a habit of knowing where everyone was supposed to be and when. This can actually be annoying, since we tended to forget things and Kirstin would remind us. But it was helpful, too. Every morning, Kirstin is up by 5:30, even on Wednesdays and Sundays when she doesn't have to go to work. She is showered and ready shortly after that and has her breakfast at the same time each day. Whatever chores she has are rapidly dispatched, and she is always ready to go when she is supposed to. That kind of perfection is frustrating for the rest of us, who seem to always be running behind. I can't help but envy her structure and order, an impossibility for me.

KIRSTIN'S SIDE OF THE STORY

I didn't like being called Bratinella. My brother was the real brat. I didn't like it when he gave me a hard time or tried to get me to fight with him. I remember my imaginary friends a little, but I remember my real friends a lot more. At times I do talk to myself like other people do.

I'm always organized. It helps me remember. I get up at 5:30. I have breakfast. On Monday and Saturday I have Eggo waffles. Tuesdays I have Pop-Tarts. Wednesdays and Sundays, my days off, are egg days. Thursdays I have cereal, and on Fridays, I have Jimmy Dean sandwiches. After breakfast I get showered and dressed. Then I do my chores. On Mondays I wash clothes. Tuesdays I sweep my floors. Wednesday I change my sheets, clean my bathroom, wash sheets and towels, and water my plants. Thursdays and Saturdays there are no chores to do. On Fridays I dust and take the trash cans out to the curb. Every day I help my grandmother with whatever she needs me to do. On Wednesdays, one of my parents takes me shopping at Walmart. I buy groceries for my grandmother and me. I always take bags to put our groceries in. This helps save the environment from too many plastic bags. When we get home, I put the groceries away. Every night I set the table and help my grandmother with dinner. Then I do the dishes.

Chapter Five

"One, We Are the Girls!"

The mother-daughter relationship is a special kind of phenomenon that is difficult to explain. It is a relationship that changes over time but remains an important part of a woman's life. The father-daughter relationship is also wonderful, but mothers and daughters can share a kind of intimacy that fathers can't easily grasp. With Kirstin and me, we have shared a special bond that I believe began with caring for her in the hospital when she had meningitis. It was strengthened further during the time we spent together when she was in preschool. There has never been a time when Kirstin and I haven't been friends. I know that many mothers and daughters go through rough periods, where they struggle to define their respective roles. Kirstin and I struggled a little, but I consider it one of the trade-offs that her teen years were pleasant ones. This is especially amazing when you consider that besides being her mother, I was her teacher during four years of high school.

Craig and Michael always seemed to be busy with work or scouting, doing guy things. So Kirstin and I spent a lot of time together. We played games and Barbies and read stories. We developed our own cheer. It was adapted from one of the cheers performed at the football games for the high school where I teach. It went, "One, we are the girls. Two, we do it right. Three, we are number one . . . We are the girls." If this bothered Craig or Michael, they never said so. Kirstin's favorite nightgown bore the words, "Girls are great. Girls are dynamite. Girls are fantastic. Boys stink." We laughed about it and recited the words. We were the girls.

I only recall a few times when Kirstin was really upset with me. The year I was the Region Eight vice president of the Jaycee Women, I traveled quite a bit to the seven states I was in charge of helping. On one trip to Denver, Colorado, Michael was able to go with me and spend some time with my cousin, Connie, who has a son exactly one month younger than Kirstin. After my meetings, Michael and I stayed with the Colorado Jaycee Women president in Boulder at her little ranch on a creek. It was a fun and relaxing time for both of us. My next trip was to New Mexico, and Craig and Kirstin were seeing me off at the airport. Kirstin was about five at the time but small enough that Craig was holding her in his arms. Kirstin had somehow gotten the idea that since Michael had gone with me on the previous trip, this was her turn to go along with Mom. When she realized that wasn't going to happen, she turned her head away and refused to tell me good-bye. When I returned from my trip, she still wasn't talking to me.

Another time, we were eating in a restaurant. It was during Kirstin's "Little Mermaid" period (which she has never grown out of). We were looking at our menus and trying to decide what to order. When I suggested that I might have the flounder, Kirstin shot me a dirty look. Deciding that was what I wanted anyway, I tried to whisper my selection to our server. Kirstin still heard, and I was on her list for the rest of the day.

Sometimes Kirstin and I would plan a surprise for Craig and Michael. We might bake some chocolate chip cookies or learn a new song. Our surprises didn't always turn out as planned. Once we were working on a riddle Kirstin would ask her father when he came home from work. All afternoon she practiced, "What's green on the inside, white on the outside, and hops?" She had it down pat and was so excited that when she heard Craig at the door, she went running to him. "Dad, Dad, I've got a joke, a frog sandwich."

All of Kirstin's dolls were real people. They had names and personalities. Kirstin had two Cabbage Patch dolls, which came with names and birth certificates. Both times we had to fill out adoption papers and send them in to change the dolls' names, because Kirstin was not satisfied with the ones they had been given. The first one she named Sherry. Sherry had her own song—"Sherry Baby," by Frankie Valle. Kirstin would sing to her doll and dance her around. Her second Cabbage Patch doll was dressed like a clown, and she named him Charlie Brown. Of course his song was Buck Owens's, "Charlie Brown, He's a Clown."

Kirstin's absolute favorite doll of all time was Paula. She was a baby doll with a voice box that was activated by motion. Paula didn't talk; she made baby sounds that seemed real. She accompanied us everywhere, including our trip to Hawaii. Paula was in an infant carrier, and once when we were waiting at the airport to fly to another island, I was holding Paula upside down in her carrier under my arm. A woman came over to check it out. When she realized Paula was just a doll, she said, "I couldn't imagine you were holding a baby like that." But to Kirstin, Paula was a real baby.

Every night Paula went to sleep with Kirstin. The problem was that whenever Kirstin moved, Paula would wake up. First she would coo and make baby sounds, but if no one picked her up, she would start crying. Eventually, we figured out that we could remove the voice box after Kirstin went to sleep. Paula was Kirstin's companion from five years old until she started high school.

I sewed most of Kirstin's clothes and also made outfits for her dolls. A fabric store was going out of business, and I was able to buy dozens of patterns for Kirstin that included a small pattern for a Cabbage Patch doll. There were iron-on decals and everything. Pretty soon, Kirstin and Sherry Baby had a huge wardrobe. One year for Easter, I was able to make matching dresses for the three of us.

Each summer, the local movie theater had a weekly children's movie. This became our summer ritual, and every week Kirstin, Sherry Baby, and I would go to the movies. Kirstin and Sherry always wore matching outfits, and the workers at the theater would watch for us and say, "Here they come." Due to Kirstin's maturity level, she enjoyed the types of movies they were showing, so we continued with this routine much longer than most moms and daughters would. We called it our "girls' day out."

One birthday, Kirstin insisted she wanted a Doctor Barbie. Nothing else would do. Toy shopping in June was not an easy task in our town in those days. K-mart and other stores only had a large selection of toys at Christmastime. The rest of the year there were just a few aisles. No one seemed to have a Doctor Barbie, and I was down to one possibility. There was a toy store in town. Their prices were pretty high, but that was still cheaper than going to Phoenix. To my relief, they had a Doctor Barbie.

At her birthday party, Kirstin opened her presents. She became most excited when she saw the Doctor Barbie. "I have a Doctor Barbie," she squealed, "Now I have someone to fix Ken's leg." Her Ken doll, it seemed, had lost his leg, and Kirstin's solution to fixing it was getting a Doctor Barbie.

Never able to think of Kirstin in any way other than "normal," I devised my own way of looking at things. I decided that I could think of Kirstin as a developmentally delayed six-year-old or a precocious four-year-old. I decided to think of her as the latter, and, of course, her small size helped in my deception. I'm not sure how much influence my little mind games had on my decisions concerning Kirstin, but it affected my attitude nonetheless.

Another experience Kirstin and I shared was Camp Fire Boys and Girls. When we first began, Kirstin's speech therapist was the leader, and I was her helper. She had two boys, so it was a boys and girls club. We had meetings, went on camping trips, and earned emblems. There were gatherings at the camp, which was located nearby, and we got together with other groups. This was a great opportunity for Kirstin to be with typical kids, and she was accepted as one of the group.

When our speech therapist took a job in Phoenix, I became the leader, and we switched to a group for girls only. Every week we had meetings at our house, and we worked on projects related to wilderness, crafts, and hobbies. One thing I learned from this experience was that Kirstin didn't really have any more problems completing the projects than any of the other members. They all seemed to have skills that came easily to them and others that were more difficult. That was also true of Kirstin, who was capable of doing the same things as other girls her age. She was not the child I stood by when we did crafts to make sure she didn't have it upside down or backward. There was always someone else having more problems, and Kirstin was doing fine all by herself.

As a fund-raiser every year, Camp Fire members sold candy and nuts. We always set a goal and worked together to meet it. The girls sold door to door if their parents permitted it, and we also set up tables in front of banks and stores. Kirstin proved to be an excellent saleslady. After all, who could say no to that angelic face? Going around the neighborhood with her, I stayed at the curb and let her transact the sale on her own. She managed just fine, making the sale and collecting money.

Every year we used the proceeds from our candy sale to go on a trip. One year we went camping in Sedona. There were lots of hiking and Camp Fire activities, as well as a trip to the local fish hatchery. That was our last stop, and the girls took their catches home so someone else could clean the fish. Another time, we stayed in a hotel in Phoenix. We went swimming, ice-skating, and visited the Pioneer Living History Museum. This gave Kirstin another opportunity to be with typical kids her own age and gave me a chance to see that Kirstin was just like other girls her age in a lot of ways.

Another typical experience for Kirstin was summer camp. Growing up, I had been a Camp Fire Girl, and so had my mother. Kirstin's grandmother had attended Camp Womatochick as a girl, and so had my sister and I. Now Kirstin was going to the same camp. We packed her gear and met the bus bringing the other campers up from Phoenix. Once Kirstin was on the bus, for a week, she was just like any other camper. She had to take care of her own needs, make decisions, handle chores, ride horses, and go on long hikes. And she did them all in true Kirstin fashion . . . give her a challenge and she'll meet it head-on.

There was one time-honored experience the parents of little girls must face sooner or later. That is the slumber party. Kirstin had her share of those. Anyone who has daughters knows what I'm talking about when I say little girls talk nonstop. Put together seven or eight of them, and they can drive you to your bedroom for some peace. Why it's called a slumber party is a mystery to me, as no sleeping takes place.

When we moved to Prescott Valley, Kirstin was just turning eight years old. In Chandler, they were beginning to talk to us about Special Olympics, but we moved away before Kirstin was old enough, since the beginning age is eight. There was no organized group in Prescott Valley, but we really wanted Kirstin to have the experience. Of course our solution was to start a group here. At the time, there was a self-contained class at Lake Valley Elementary and also at Humboldt Middle School. I talked to the teachers at both schools about training the athletes at our schools. Dorothy Mobley was all for it. Kirstin was in her class and would be participating. The middle-school teacher wasn't able to fully participate, so we arranged for the middle-schoolers to come up to the high school to train. This worked out well for me, because I was able to get to know some of the students who would soon be in my class.

There was no equipment for us to use, not even a measuring tape. I had a meter stick that I used to mark off fifty meters and one hundred meters on the dirt track around our football field. Later, when we decided to run the relay, I had to have four one hundred-meter distances marked off. This was backbreaking work, going around the track, measuring one meter at a time. Still, that was all we needed except for the stopwatch I borrowed from the PE department. The other event we chose was the softball throw, because it was easy to round up some softballs, also from the PE department.

The first two years, everyone was entered in a racing event and softball throw. We trained twice a week to get ready for the area games in Cottonwood. All our athletes were there with their parents, and we made a fairly decent showing for our first year.

After the area games, we went on to the Arizona State Games. I was able to get a school van, and the trainers—including some high school students who helped out—and athletes rode down in that. Some of the parents also went down in their own vehicles. Arizona Special Olympics paid for the rooms for athletes and trainers as well as provided our meals.

One thing I learned about Kirstin through these competitions surprised me: she was not a good sport. I soon learned that she would never be one of those self-sacrificing Special Olympics athletes you read about or see in movies. You know—the one who is way out ahead until another athlete falls down. Suddenly, amid cries of "Keep going," this very loving person, who has the race won, turns around to help his fallen comrade. Kirstin would probably step right over that person on her way to the finish line. More than once she embarrassed me by getting angry when she did not win. She always wanted to win.

After we moved to Prescott Valley, Kirstin continued to do gymnastics at Mile High gymnastics. When we were getting the information on Special Olympics from the state, I asked for the rules for gymnastics. Kirstin's instructor at Mile High was willing to work with her on the routines. She would be doing the vault, balance beam, and floor exercises. Every athlete had to do the same routines. The floor routine was to the theme song from "St. Elmo's Fire." I called it the song you learn to hate, because we played it over and over as Kirstin practiced her routine.

There were no area games for gymnastics in northern Arizona; in fact, Kirstin may have been the only athlete. So she was allowed to go directly to the state games without competing at a lower level. The state games were intimidating, with so many athletes and events. We were all alone and just learning what to do. Kirstin did her best, of course, but came away with no medals.

The balance beam was Kirstin's most difficult event, because her balance was not good. She had enough trouble staying on the beam let alone performing tricks on it. She never gave up, and eventually she began earning medals, sometimes in all three events.

When we moved to Chino Valley, we helped organize the Special Olympics there. The other parents were interested in adding gymnastics as an event for all our athletes. There were a couple of reasons gymnastics was appealing. First of all, the competition took place in an air-conditioned gym. In Tempe, Arizona, in May, that was something to be coveted. The second reason was the number of events. The athletes competing in track and field could only compete in two events. Gymnastics counted as a single event, no matter how many different parts of it you competed in. Our athletes competed in the same three: balance beam, vault, and floor. That gave them three chances for medals, and they could still compete in track and field.

Another mom and I became the coaches. She had gymnastics experience as a child. I didn't, but I knew the routines from helping Kirstin. We were able to use the gym at Del Rio school in the afternoon and also use their equipment. It was fun having someone to practice with, and now we were a real team. When we went to the state games, we went as a team and competed that way. We supported and cheered for each other.

The Olympics has its famous gymnasts, like Mary Lou Retton or Shawn Johnson. Arizona Special Olympics also had a star. Her name was Christie Todd. When it was her turn to perform, everyone stopped to watch. Her skill was amazing!

I have always made fun of those pageant moms, who push their little girls into competitions to feed their own egos. I certainly never thought of myself as that kind of a mom, but we all have our weak moments. Kirstin had been performing the same floor exercise for several years and could do it with her eyes closed. I decided one year that she should add a fourth event, original floor exercise. We developed a routine around the song "Part of Your World," from Disney's *Little Mermaid*.

As Kirstin practiced her two routines, I noticed that she was even having difficulty with the old one she knew so well. This should have been a sign to me that I was asking too much, but I didn't pay attention. Or maybe I didn't want to. At the state games, Kirstin would perform the required floor exercise with her team and then later perform the optional routine with other gymnasts. The regular floor exercise was a disaster. She was confused, left out steps, and added some of the steps from the other routine. By the time she did the optional routine, she was even more unsure of herself. Later, I apologized to Kirstin for acting like a stage mom and pushing her too far. As always, she told me not to worry about it. We hugged each other and said, "There's always next year."

Kirstin eventually moved on to other track-and-field events. She tried running long jump with some success. It was during that event at the state games when Kirstin and I met the governor of Arizona, Rose Moffart. She introduced herself and talked with Kirstin for a while, wishing her luck. Eventually, Kirstin traded the softball throw for shot put and the hundred-meter dash for race walking. These were the events the older participants chose. She was also on the bowling team for several years. Once she started working, Special Olympics was no longer possible, because her schedule did not permit her to attend the practices. Still, we have fond memories of those days together.

The Arizona Special Olympics track-and-field events take place in early May, which is already a hot time in Phoenix. One year, though, it was unseasonably cool. We had packed expecting the heat and were not prepared for the very chilly evenings. Kirstin didn't have a jacket or sweater, so we decided we should try to buy her one. Trying to buy a jacket in Phoenix in May is like trying to find an ice cream vendor at the North Pole. We went everywhere to no avail. Before the opening ceremonies, there was a tailgate party. We got there just in time for a drawing. The prize, of course, was a pink Chevrolet jacket. And, of course, Kirstin was the lucky winner. She needed a jacket, and we should have known that somehow one would be provided.

All her life, things have worked out like that for Kirstin. I attribute it to a remarkable guardian angel. At a picnic in Awatukee, Arizona, Kirstin climbed to the top of a big slide. Craig and I were watching from below, and we saw her fall. Everyone else who saw her saw the same thing we did. Kirstin wafted down like a feather. When she hit the ground, we ran to her. Nothing was broken; in fact, there was not a scratch on her. To this day, Kirstin avoids slides, but in my mind, her landing was nothing short of a miracle.

As I said before, Kirstin was my student through four years of high school. Those were special years for us. Because we lived in Chino, there was a thirty-minute drive each way every day. This was our time to spend together talking, laughing, and planning. Sometimes we would study for a test, or Kirstin would practice her speech homework. But for that time, we could relax and enjoy just being together.

Kirstin had been out of high school a few years when I took her and my mother to the Women's Expo at the Phoenix Civic Center. We had watched the ads on TV and were very excited about attending. One of the first things we saw there was a large stage with a salon set up by a well-known hairstylist. On the TV news every Monday morning, he and his helpers performed miracle makeovers for a deserving group of women—women trying to reenter the workforce, women who were in the military, etc.

We watched for a while as a stylist finished giving a haircut and then selected someone from the audience to be the next to receive a free hairstyling. Kirstin was very excited about the prospect of having her hair styled by a professional, so she waited patiently as one after another, the people in front of her were chosen. Once she was near the front, she began waving her arms, asking to be next. The ladies around her joined in and pointed at her, saying, "Pick her." Unfortunately, the stylists looked over Kirstin's head and chose women standing behind her. After a while, we figured out that they were avoiding Kirstin on purpose. Not wanting to let that ruin our day, we gave up and moved on to look at the exhibits. "Why did they do that?" Kirstin asked as much to herself as to me. I had no answer for her. How do you explain prejudice? It's possible they had a bad experience with someone with disabilities. I should give them the benefit of the doubt. But isn't that what prejudice is—making up your mind about someone based on a single characteristic? Kirstin is so much more than a person with Down syndrome.

The highlight of our day was getting to meet Catherine Hicks of the television series *7th Heaven*. She spoke to the crowd about growing up in Arizona and about her acting career. She talked about the cast of *7th Heaven* and how much she enjoyed being a part of it. When Ms. Hicks finished speaking, she invited members of the audience to ask questions. Microphones had been set up for that purpose. Kirstin had a question she wanted to ask, but I tried to discourage her. Fearing an embarrassing moment for both of us, I told her to wait and see if someone else might ask her question. Of course, no one did, and the next thing I knew, Kirstin was walking up to the microphone, which seemed to be a mile away. At the microphone, she did not hesitate but spoke right up. "How did you like playing opposite Tony Danza in *She's Out of Control*?" Catherine Hicks responded to her question by talking about how much fun it was to make that movie. Later, when we were able to meet Ms. Hicks personally, she commented on how Kirstin has asked such a good question.

Kirstin and I still enjoy having a girls' day out. Most of the time they consist of a shopping trip to Walmart. But recently I treated Kirstin to an Amy Grant concert. It was her "2-Friends" tour with Michael W. Smith. Kirstin has been a fan of Amy Grant since high school, maybe even longer. She has all of her CDs and knows all of her songs. She has read her biography. Kirstin has been to Amy Grant and Vince Gill concerts, but this one was special. Being paired with Michael W. Smith, we knew Amy Grant would be singing her Christian songs. Tim's Toyota Center was filled with believers. Here and there around the stadium, people were standing, praising God, and singing along. Next to me stood Kirstin, hands raised, swaying to the music, lost in her own private worship of her Lord. How I wanted to be her at that moment as I sat motionless, clutching my purse in my lap. When everyone rose in applause, I joined them, but otherwise, I stayed in my seat. *Why couldn't I be like Kirstin?* I wondered. She was free to act on her feelings, while I was paralyzed by my own fear of appearing foolish. After all these years, I still have much to learn from my beautiful daughter.

KIRSTIN'S SIDE OF THE STORY

Mom forgot to mention some of my favorite dolls. I had a Rainbow Bright doll. Mom made me a costume, and I was Rainbow Bright for Halloween. (Note from Mom: It had fifty-seven pattern pieces.) I had a lot of Barbies, Skippers, and Ken dolls. I had the Barbie Dreamhouse, Corvette, and motor home. I also had all of the New Kids on the Block and Barbie and the Rockers.

I love dolls and collect them. I have Baby-Sitter's Club dolls and American Girl dolls. My first American Girl doll was Kirsten Larsen. She is a pioneer girl. Her birthday is June 8, and mine is June 9. My other American Girl dolls are Samantha, Molly, and Josephina. I didn't play with those dolls, except Kirsten. Mom made clothes for her, and I have some of her accessories.

Mom said that I wasn't a good sport at Special Olympics. I did mess up there, but I learned that winning isn't everything. Now I'm a good sport and a team player. I liked Special Olympics bowling the best. I have lots of trophies. I have my own bowling ball. It is pink and has my name on it. I made a lot of friends in Special Olympics, and I like being a part of a team. At work I am part of a team. Special Olympics helped me with that.

One of the things I did with Mom was Horses with Heart. My parents had two horses—Suzie and Pepper. I didn't ride them. I did ride at Horses with Hearts. It was fun. One time I was in the Exceptional Rodeo, but they had fake horses.

I like spending time with both my parents. Sometimes we invite our guys, Dad, and my fiancé David, to come along. We go to movies and lunch on a double date. Sometimes we go hiking or bowling. I look forward to going on a girls' day out with my mom. In fact, we had one today. We went shopping at the mall. I bought some cute clothes. Mom helped me pick them out. We went to lunch and then to Walmart to buy my groceries. I hope we never get too old for a girls' day out.

Chapter Six

ಶಿ ೧೫

Teaching the Teacher

I've heard Dr. Phil talk about an "aha moment," one of those times in a person's life that will always be remembered, because it was at that very moment something life-altering occurred. I had one of those moments in 1979. Kirstin was attending the regular preschool, and her teacher and I were having trouble communicating about her progress. Flo suggested that we keep a notebook at the preschool. She would write in it each day, and so would I.

Every day, I wrote about Kirstin's accomplishments. "Today Kirstin asked a question. Kirstin helped make her bed. Now Kirstin can put on her shoes."

As I have said, Kirstin's attendance in the regular preschool pointed out many areas where she fell behind. Every day Flo would write about something Kirstin had trouble with. "Today Kirstin wouldn't participate with the other children. Kirstin had trouble using scissors. It is hard for Kirstin to color inside the lines."

Every day I read Flo's comments and felt more and more frustrated. One day after reading all of the things that Kirstin couldn't do that day, I wrote, "Isn't there anything Kirstin can do?" That was my aha moment. It was at that moment I decided to become a special education teacher. I would focus on what students were able to do and use that to build upon. That way we would focus on the positive not on the negative. If you can learn one thing, I surmised, you can learn more, and there's no way to tell how far that can take us. That has stayed my teaching philosophy for twenty-nine years.

At home that night, I told Craig of my plan to go back to college to study special education. I already had a degree in secondary education and had taught reading for a year in a middle school before having my son. Teaching had always been my love, and I was eager to return to it. Craig was supportive and patient as I went through the process of being accepted into a graduate program at Arizona State University.

Going back to school wasn't easy. I was teaching at a small Christian school. Michael was eight, and Kirstin was just four years old. Since the classes I was taking were graduate-level ones, they were offered in the evenings and at various locations; some were even on television at five o'clock in the morning. It was difficult to keep up with everything, so I quit my job and devoted my time (minus family time) to getting my special education certification. I had no financial aid, which meant I had to pay for each class I took. I couldn't believe how much college tuition had gone up in the nine years since I earned by bachelor's degree.

I had also forgotten what a nightmare registering for classes was. On one occasion, I took six-year-old Kirstin with me. We had been standing in a line that only seemed to move every ten or fifteen minutes. After about an hour, Kirstin asked, "Mom, is this the girls' line or the boys' line?" Of course that caused a ripple of laughter down the row of students and provided some much-needed comic relief.

It was during my course work in special education I had another experience that contributed to what would later become my teaching philosophy. One of my professors had worked at the Coolidge facility and related this story to us. He was looking in on some of the residents, and while he was there, he told a joke to the nurses. They didn't get the joke, but a woman with cerebral palsy laughed. Her cerebral palsy was so severe that she could not move her arms or legs, nor could she speak. Confined to a bed or wheelchair, she required constant care as if she were a baby.

The fact that she laughed intrigued my professor, so he decided to try a little experiment. Arranging the room so she could not see him, he told another joke. Again she laughed. This was repeated, and in every instance, she laughed at the appropriate time. Certain that her brain activity was much more than anyone knew (people with cerebral palsy can have average intelligence and above), he decided to develop a program so that she would be able to communicate and learn.

Before he could put his plan into effect, the family of this woman took her home for Christmas. While she was there, she developed pneumonia and died. It struck me as so tragic that, for her entire life, she had been unable to express to others the extent of her understanding of what was going on around her. And now that someone had discovered the truth about her, it was too late. That story has stayed with me, and it is the reason why I never give up on a single student. How do I know if the next thing I try will be the answer?

As I studied about various causes and conditions of mental retardation, I also learned that what I was dealing with as a parent of a child with a mental disability was nothing compared to what some parents lived with each day. I have the greatest respect for parents of children with disabilities. They devote so much time and make huge sacrifices in their lives, and they do it all with great love. All of my students have amazing parents.

Finally, by the end of second semester in 1983, I had finished enough of my program to get an elementary and special education certification. After completing an internship at a middle school, I was ready to start applying for a job. My certification allowed me to teach students with mild disabilities from kindergarten through high school, but I felt more comfortable with the older students. I had just begun to think about applying when we decided to move to Prescott Valley.

This was a very small, rural community, and getting a teaching job was going to be a challenge. Fortunately for me, however, the Humboldt Unified School District was expanding its special education department and needed to hire two teachers for their new self-contained programs. That was where I met Dorothy Mobley, who had also just earned her teaching certificate and moved to Prescott Valley. One of the job openings was at the elementary school, and the other was at the high school. Since Kirstin was going to be attending the elementary school, Dorothy was given that job, and I was assigned to the high school. Of course I had no problem with that assignment.

Nothing in my teacher training prepared me for my first day as the new special education teacher at Bradshaw Mountain High School. There were six students who were considered to be in the self-contained program. They did not have their own teacher but were assigned to the resource teacher, who had a separate class to teach. The students in the self-contained class were being taught by an aide in an adjoining room. That is until I got there.

At least I had my own classroom, but that was about all I had. There were some desks, an old sofa, and a few paperback workbooks. The aide had made some flash cards. My students spent most of the day in the classroom, including lunchtime. They did go to a homemaking class one semester and a woodshop class the second semester. These were special classes for my students only. Some of my students went to regular PE. It seemed I had my work cut out for me. The first change I made was with lunch—no more eating in the classroom. We went to the cafeteria like everyone else. We also attended pep assemblies and all of the other school activities. We became a part of the campus community.

The special education director allowed me to order some materials, and little by little, I built a program. There was no curriculum for me to go by, no course of study, not even a list of objectives. There was not even any subject matter to be covered. I thought about what my students would need to survive after high school and based my instruction on that.

I had to overcome some challenges before my class was running smoothly. First of all, my students weren't used to being instructed by a teacher, and the aide wasn't used to being told what to do by a teacher. After some months, they accepted my role as the leader of the class but not without a few bumps in the road.

In my new class I had one student with Down syndrome, a bright and happy young lady named Candra. Before I arrived, she seemed to have everyone convinced that she had a seizure disorder. When there was work to do and she didn't want to do it, she had a seizure. I wondered how anyone had been fooled, but then they didn't have the experience I had with my own little actress. It took me a short while to convince everyone that she was not having seizures. I said, "Watch how her eyes flutter. People who are having seizures don't do that."

Once Candra learned the seizure scam would no longer work, she resorted to temper tantrums. I recall one class period where we were all working, and she was in the back of the classroom, lying on some mats, kicking at the filing cabinet, and sobbing loudly. The noise was disruptive, but my other students were very good. We went on with our lesson and totally ignored Candra. What she didn't know was that I had developed a system that included prizes for the students who accumulated a number of points. At the end of the class, I passed out the point sheets and let everyone mark down their ten points. Now Candra was quiet and interested in the points. "Why don't I get any points?" she demanded to know.

"Because you didn't do your work," was my answer.

That was all it took and that was the end of the seizures. I had to thank Kirstin and the lesson she taught me with her restaurant scam. Score another victory for me. My sense of accomplishment was short-lived however. A few weeks later, the girls PE teacher came to me very concerned about an incident that had occurred involving Candra. The bus routes required some students to get off of one bus at the middle school and get on another to go to the high school. That morning, Candra claimed, when she was at the middle school, some students there pushed her around and took her PE clothes. The PE teacher was really upset, but I told her I would handle it. It only took me a few minutes to get Candra to admit that she had made up the whole story because she forgot her PE clothes. She could fool some of the teachers, but she was learning that I wasn't one of them. Eventually, Candra accepted my role as the teacher and her role as a student, and we became friends.

Those were the fun days of teaching for me. While I did my best to fill our days with meaningful activities, we had time to take walks around the campus and get to know each other. I thought my students were bright and capable, with charming personalities. Parents were supportive and pleased that there was a teacher just for their children. I was still finishing my master's program, which involved driving to Phoenix once or twice a week for classes. But somehow we managed to get everything done.

Now that I was teaching full time, Kirstin was introduced to a new experience: day care. Every morning before school, I dropped her off at the only nursery in town. From there she caught the bus to school. After school, the bus brought her back to Busy Bee, and I picked her up there on my way home. One day as I arrived at Busy Bee, they sent out the three daughters of one of my coworkers. I quickly informed them that I had brought one child in, and I was only taking one child home. Apparently there was some confusion, because we were both special education teachers and both blond. Still, we weren't interchangeable as teachers or as parents.

On another occasion, I came to pick up Kirstin and was told that she wasn't there. I had left her with them in the morning and expected her to be there in the afternoon. But she hadn't been on the bus when it arrived from school. No one had called me to find out why she wasn't on the bus, and no one had any idea where she was. After calling the school, I started driving around the streets of our small town. The transportation department also sent drivers out to try to find Kirstin, but all to no avail. She wasn't anywhere.

Finally, I thought that it would be a good idea to see if she was at home. This didn't seem too likely to me, because it meant that she would have to get on a bus that she didn't normally ride without being detected by teachers, aides, or bus drivers. As I drove into our driveway, I noticed the door on our camp trailer was slightly open. As I walked up to the trailer, Kirstin came out. She had somehow determined the correct bus to take to our house, managed to get on the bus and get off at exactly the right bus stop, and to walk the rest of the way home. While I was upset with her for putting me through such terror, I had to admire her ingenuity.

People were moving into our community, and our high school began to grow. That meant more students for me. Also, Mayer, a nearby town, didn't have a self-contained program like ours. They were trying to provide for those students just like my district had before I came. Since they only had three students, busing them to our school seemed like a very good solution to their problem. And so my class began to grow.

The popular teaching method at the time was thematic units, and that was an easy way for me to incorporate reading, math, and workplace skills into one activity. We would operate a nursery business. The first step was to prepare a proposal, which we submitted to the special education director. We took a trip to a nursery for help in getting started and learned that we needed plants, seeds, pots, trays, grow lights, potting soil, and tools. Using the prices we had written down, we prepared our budget to be included in the proposal. The total was just over one hundred dollars.

While we were waiting to find out if our proposal was accepted, we prepared the classroom and discussed how we would divide the labor. The class decided to rotate the jobs so that everyone would have experience at each job. Some students would take cuttings and plant them, others would take care of the plants and water them, and the third group would be the sales staff. We had permission to sell our plants in the cafeteria. Our profits went into the Special Olympics account. The project was a great success, and we learned about growing and caring for plants, making a budget, and sales techniques.

Selling plants to other students didn't turn out to be our best idea, but we were able to raise a little money. The teachers and staff were our best customers. Since we did not have to repay the hundred dollars, our sales were 100 percent profit. We saved the money and used it for our Special Olympics club.

In addition to working on academic skills, I knew my students needed experiences outside of our campus. I was able to take my entire class on outings to the few businesses we had in our town. A man with big dreams had a very small amusement park that he called Welch's

Mountain Fantasy. He was very insistent that I bring my class there. Eventually I did, and he treated them to rides on his train and a spaceship that moved back and forth. The owner seemed nervous the entire time we were there, and I wondered if he was afraid we would break something. Still, it was a fun outing. Later I was able to arrange a day-long trip to Sunset Crater. We were treated to a view of the crater from a higher vantage point on a nearby mountain. We explored the surrounding area and watched the seismograph. We were even given a personal tour of an ice cave. Everyone was outfitted with a hard hat, and we climbed around through the tight spaces of the cave. From there we went to the nearby Wupatki Indian ruins for an added adventure. This was a trip I was able to provide again with other classes of students.

With smaller groups of students, I was able to arrange some specific opportunities. One of my friends lived nearby, and she provided day care for a small group of children. I managed to take two students at a time to help her. We planned activities that we would do with the children there and brought snacks we made in home economics class. Everyone seemed to enjoy the experience, including my friend who had a welcome break.

I have seen great benefits from taking my students on field trips. We have gone to the Phoenix Zoo, Out of Africa, the Pioneer Living History Museum, as well as the Arizona Science Center, the Challenger Museum, and the Renaissance Festival. In addition to trips to Sunset Crater, we have gone to other national parks, including the Grand Canyon. Some of my students are fortunate enough to be able to go to such places with their families, but others are not. In keeping with the promise we made when Kirstin was a preschooler, we have taken her everywhere. It is surprising to me that some families choose to keep their specially challenged children at home, especially considering that they are eligible for a Golden Access card from the National Parks Service. This card not only gets the person with a disability into the park free of charge but also allows the entire carload of friends or family to get in free as well.

Special Olympics was something we looked forward to with great anticipation. First, there would be the area games in Cottonwood and then the state games at Arizona State University. For most of my students, this was their only opportunity to travel away from home and stay in a hotel without their parents. Taking them was a big responsibility, and I enlisted as much help as I could. Craig went along to chaperone the boys. My aide, Carolyn, and I took care of the girls. The events started on Thursday afternoon with the relay races. There were events on Friday and Saturday. Friday night was the opening ceremonies, with the parade of athletes and the lighting of the torch.

It was always difficult to get everyone to their events. Our son, Michael, who was always working on Boy Scout patches, was able to help with that. I would put him in charge of one athlete who needed supervision and a buddy. Michael would keep him entertained but also make sure he arrived at his events on time.

On Saturday afternoon, we all walked over to the ball fields for the softball throw. It was quite a hike across a main street, and we were usually dying from the heat by the time we got there. Tents were set up for us to wait in, and that was a little cooler. But after everyone finished the event, we were facing another hot walk back. That was why, on one occasion, when Candra started having one of her "attacks," I didn't really try too hard to stop her. The paramedics came to check her out and decided she was overheated. Instead of the long walk back, Candra and I rode in the nice, air-conditioned ambulance.

After dinner on Saturday, there were closing ceremonies and a dance. The dance was one of the high points of the weekend. It was a chance to get to know some of the athletes from other schools. It was also an opportunity for me to relax and have some fun with my students.

Eventually we added bowling as another Special Olympics event. We practiced at the bowling alley in our community every Saturday. After several fund-raising activities, we were able to purchase bowling balls and bags for all our athletes. This helped quite a bit, as most of them needed lighter balls and the finger holes were drilled for small children. With their own balls, bowling scores went up.

We had area games in our local bowling alley, but state games were in Tucson. This required a four-hour drive for a weekend of bowling and fun. I was able to get a fifteen-passenger van from the school district. It was an old, red van that shook and rattled like a tin can full of rocks, but it always got us there. Sometimes I had help on the trip from Craig or an aide, but there were years when it was just me and five or six of my students.

Arizona Special Olympics paid for our room, and the meals were donated by local organizations. That meant driving around to various locations in Tucson. Breakfast was provided by one organization. After the bowling tournament, lunch was provided at the bowling center. Dinner was held somewhere else, and breakfast the next day was at still another location in Tucson. Fortunately, the locations tended to be the same from year to year, so I soon learned the routine. After the tournament came the fun. We were provided with passes to many of the tourist locations in Tucson. This included Old Tucson, the Sonoran Desert Museum, and Reed Park Zoo. Sometimes we would go to the mall or roller-skating. I will never forget driving that old, red van down the steep, winding road to Old Tucson with Candra's fingernails dug into the back of my seat as she gasped, "Mrs. Heddens . . . Mrs. Heddens . . . Mrs. Heddens," in my ear all the way down to the bottom of the road.

Transition from high school to adult life was not something that anyone talked about when I began teaching special education. I did have to prepare an Individual Educational Plan (IEP) for each student with the help of the parents and therapists. As I mentioned earlier, the IEP contained a list of goals to be worked on during the coming school year and the services that would be provided by the school district. In those days, IEPs were only a few pages long, and there was no section called "Transition." In spite of that, transition was what was foremost on parents' minds. They all knew that sooner or later, public school would end, and they would be trying to figure out what to do next.

One of my first students to graduate from high school and leave my class was Candra. Her parents worked, so she would be home alone all day. There were many problems with this, but they were excellent parents, who took things one problem at a time. The first area of concern was Candra's love of food. If left on her own, she would eat whatever was in the house. Her parents solved this by locking up the food except what was in a small ice chest. That was Candra's daily allotment. She could eat it all first thing in the morning or spread her eating out over the course of the day; that was up to her. This was a wonderful solution, and it worked.

Some of the concepts I had taught in my class caused problems for Candra's family. For one thing, we had a session on government in which we discussed the basic points of the US Constitution. Apparently this did not fall on deaf ears where Candra was concerned. One day when two policemen came to her door, she asked to see their paper (search warrant). When they told her they didn't have a paper, she slammed the door in their faces. At other times, she called the police herself. When they arrived, she would ask them to adjust the thermostat or get something that she needed.

When her boyfriend's grandmother was in the hospital, Candra called the police to tell them about it. They weren't sure what she was saying but only understood that someone was dying. Police cars, ambulances, and fire trucks were dispatched to her home immediately.

Eventually, the Arizona Department of Education started telling school districts that they had to provide transition. It has taken them many years to define just what that is, and it seems it is constantly being refined. At the beginning, it could be whatever school districts could provide. Some parents shopped around to other nearby districts, and at the parents' request, our district tuitioned their students to another school. Once there, they often found that the grass just looked greener, and pretty soon those students were back in my class. As the parent of a special needs child, I understood their desperation and did what I could to provide an adequate transition program within the limitations of our school programs and funding.

Our district eventually hired someone to help students find jobs in the community. This was somewhat successful, and several of my students were working at paying jobs when they graduated. The problem was that once the support was pulled away, they had difficulties at work, and most of them eventually lost their jobs. Students who were receiving services through the DDD fared better, as they had supports in place when they left school. It became obvious that agencies needed to work together to see that transition went as smoothly as possible.

Unfortunately, budget cuts brought an end to the work program. At different times, parents came up with their own ideas, such as paying someone to hire their teenager, but it would be several years before we had a decent vocational program.

My students today have choices when it comes to preparing for the workplace. Some of them participate in the Youth Transition Program (YTP), which works with Arizona Rehabilitative Services (ARS) to help them overcome barriers to employment. ARS is an agency within the Department of Economic Security. It provides assistance to people who have employment challenges due to a disability. This could be someone who has worked at a career, but due to injuries, the person must find a new form of employment. ARS assists that person with training or specialized equipment which will permit the worker to be employed once again. For students with special needs who are becoming adults, ARS provides comprehensive testing, college assistance, job placement and coaching, driver's education—whatever is needed for the student to be successful in the workplace.

For students who do not qualify for YTP, our high school work program provides them with a chance to try out a variety of jobs on our campus and in the community. They are paid a training wage through special education funds. The work program is paired with class work to prepare students for filling out applications, interviewing for jobs and dealing with workplace issues.

At various times we have had parents who felt it was the school's responsibility to find their child a job before graduation. Of course this is not possible. In a free enterprise system such as ours, no one is guaranteed a job, at least not in competitive employment. We have no way to make employers hire anyone, including our students with disabilities. We do our best to prepare our students for the workplace, and that is all we can promise.

What happens when high school ends depends largely on what parents are willing to do. Kirstin has been fortunate in that she has always had two parents devoted to her success. In many cases, all of the responsibility falls on the mother, who may already be overburdened with a job, a home, and other children. I love to see both parents attend an IEP meeting. It gives me confidence that this student will receive the support he or she needs. I've had many students who were being raised by their grandparents. As a grandparent myself, I feel for them. They often continue to work long after retirement age in order to support grandchildren. There are some support services for grandparents raising special grandchildren, but usually they are not nearly enough. While there are services that can help take up some of the slack when parents can't, they can never replace the dedication of two fully engaged parents.

There is another type of transition my students needed, and I worked hard to provide it. That was educational opportunities beyond my classroom, where they would have chances to interact with their nondisabled peers. One of my first attempts at mainstreaming came about when two of the young men in my class wanted to be in boys' weights. The football coach was the weights teacher, and his first reaction was fear that they might get hurt. It took some tall talking on my part and a promise to send someone to keep an eye on them in class that finally won us a trial period. As time went on, the aide was no longer needed, because the football players were more than willing to help my students learn to lift weights. Even the coach found it beneficial to have them in class. Whenever one of his players started complaining about some ache or pain, he would point to my students and say, "You see those two over there? They have more problems than you'll ever have, and you don't see them whining." Of course that was true. No matter what, you would always see a smile on their faces.

"Full inclusion" was a term that came along later. Unlike mainstreaming, full inclusion meant that the special education student would be in regular classes all day. In my twenty-nine years as a special education teacher, I have stood my ground in the middle as the pendulum has swung back and forth between being self-contained and fully included. I make sure all of my students spend part of their school day in classes other than mine. Making sure they can achieve success in their regular classes is a responsibility I take seriously. It is my belief that providing a mix of regular and special education classes removes a lot of the stress they would feel with full inclusion. Getting a modified curriculum in the extended resource classroom allows my students to focus more energy on the rigorous curriculum of their regular classes.

If a supervisor started talking to me about full inclusion, I would want to know what his or her motive is. If the supervisor is only thinking of money, I am dead set against it. Inclusion has to be more than just geography. Putting a student in a regular class because he or she can benefit from being there is different from putting the student there because it is expedient. Successful placement in regular classes requires a great deal of preparation and cooperation. It is no way to cut the budget.

The hardest behaviors I've had to eliminate were from students who had been placed in a regular class but were given alternative work to do. When I hand them a worksheet, they immediately fill in the blanks with any answer. Then they turn in their papers and are finished. When I point out that the answers are all incorrect and that we are going to do it together as a class, I meet with opposition. The student doesn't want to do the work over again. I eventually win out, and the student learns to wait and work on the assignment as I ask. But this usually takes a few weeks or even months. I am never surprised when I read about all of the behavior problems reported in the student's IEP by the previous teacher. If a student is finishing the work in a matter of a few minutes, there is plenty of time to get in trouble just to break up the boredom and monotony.

When a student isn't held accountable for having correct answers, he or she quickly learns that being correct doesn't matter. While I don't check every answer on every piece of work my students hand in, I check enough to keep them honest. I also hold them accountable for learning the material we cover in class. Every unit ends with a test. Over the years I have developed a system that enables everyone to keep up, and I give them the tools necessary to learn the material. I know what my students know and what they don't know.

While I have guarded feelings about full inclusion, I have no such reservations when it comes to what I call "reverse inclusion." What I mean by that is having the regular education students come into the special education classroom. This is a winning combination for everyone. For the students in the self-contained program, it is an opportunity to have a buddy who knows them and says "Hi" when they walk across the campus. For the typical students, they find ready-made friends who are fun to be with, never judge, and ask for nothing but their time and attention. It never comes as a surprise to see the students on a campus rally around a student with special needs as their choice for homecoming king. I have seen it happen many times. I think the students get tired of all the egos involved in such selections and want to choose someone who is kind and humble—who is truly deserving of the honor and will be the same friendly person after the event is over.

For the first half of my teaching career, my students were exempt from the standardized tests that were given each year. With the implementation of state-mandated tests and No Child Left Behind, there have been various efforts to include my students in the testing. At first, they were given the regular state test, but at their current reading level. This was not very successful and didn't provide much useful information. Because the content was written for first—or second-grade students, it was not interesting. Besides, the test covered things I didn't spend time on, since I was trying to prepare my students for adulthood.

A test was eventually devised just for students with cognitive disabilities. It has been revised and is a fairly appropriate test. Some special education teachers don't think state tests are appropriate for our students. I don't agree. I think teachers and students need to be held accountable. Without any standards, it would be easy for a special education teacher to water down the curriculum so that it required very little effort for the students to complete. I like to challenge my students as much as possible, and they always meet or exceed my expectations. I test my students all the time to see where they are and how much they have gained. That way I know I am being effective as a teacher. The state tests are based on standards, and the results of those tests are another indication of how we are doing.

It is my theory that because of state-mandated testing, there will be fewer students who are career special education students in the future. What I mean by that is more students will be able to move out of special education and back into regular education classes. Only students with cognitive disabilities qualify for alternative testing. Those students whose intellectual abilities fall within what is deemed to be within the average range are required to take the regular state-mandated tests. They are students who have been identified as having specific learning disabilities, emotional disabilities or autism. As more pressure is put of school districts to assure that these students are successful at passing the tests at each grade level, teachers are required to do a better job of preparing special students for those tests. This means that these students will be less likely to fall behind, as the special education teachers are working on the same standards as the regular education teachers. Once the students have the skills they need, returning to regular education is possible and desirable. As special education teachers we might be working ourselves out of a job, but I couldn't imagine a better outcome for our efforts.

While Special education students with milder challenges are required to take the same tests as the typical students, they are permitted certain accommodations. Accommodations are adjustments in the way the test is administered. For example, the test may be given in a small group, or the student may be permitted to use a word processor with the spell check turned off. Modifications are changes to the test itself. This could mean reducing the number of questions or changing the criteria for passing.

At one time, modifications were allowed in certain situations, but that is no longer the case, even for special education students.

Most, if not all, of the developed countries have some type of standardized testing. Accommodations are usually permitted for students with documented disabilities, but modifications are not. Special education is required by law in most developed countries, and inclusion or mainstreaming is the preferred model. One exception is Germany, where students are placed in special schools designed to meet the needs of students with a particular disability. There are special schools for students with learning disabilities, emotional challenges, physical limitations, and so on.

Many of my students come up the ranks in our district from the elementary school to the middle school, and finally to the high school. Because we live in an area with a rather transient population, I usually have two or three students who are new to our district. Our proximity to Mexico also means that I gain students who began their education in their native country. In most cases, the students from Mexico have been able to attend public school there. I did have one student who had never been to school until she was enrolled in my high school. About eight years ago, a group of special education teachers from Mexico visited our campus to observe our special education department. It is good to see that schools in Mexico are involved in providing for their students with special needs.

I also have a student who moved to Arizona from the Philippines. He told me that in his school in the Philippines, there were no special education classes for him. But his teacher gave him extra help, so he could complete his class work. He is a good student in my class and has adequate reading skills. It is encouraging to see developing countries working to meet the needs of all students in their schools. This is certainly a challenge when you consider that they have greater needs and a shortage of funding.

To be a special education teacher requires a great deal of dedication. Most if not all special education teachers have dual certification. That means we always have the option of going back into regular education.

And many teachers do go back to regular classes. The reasons vary, but it is often because of the paperwork and meetings, the demands that are placed on us, behavior problems, and stress. Those of us who remain do it because we love it. I have been told that I seem to have an unlimited amount of patience. I am very patient with my students, but that is not difficult when they are striving with all they have to accomplish something. It is easy to help them over and over again when I know they are not giving up. I have a hard time understanding how the regular education teachers can deal with students who don't even try. That would be frustrating to me. When the principal visits my class, he is always amazed that all of my students are engaged in the activities going on in my classroom. I would be amazed if they weren't.

While I am teaching my students, they are also teaching me. One of the best rewards for teaching special students is what I learn from them. They are tolerant of each other and always forgiving. Two students might be angry and arguing, and a few hours later, they are the best of friends. No matter what, they always look out for and defend one another. I have compared my class to a big family. We don't always get along, but we still love each other. If I have to discipline my class, for example, by making them stay in for five minutes of their lunchtime, they accept the punishment without complaint. No matter how many times I've witnessed that, it always surprises me.

I recall one time when I was teaching a lesson on false advertising. We were looking at an ad for a face cream. The ad claimed that the face cream would make you beautiful. As I pointed out the falsehoods in the ad, I said that a cream can't make you beautiful and that we can't all be beautiful movie stars. It seemed that my class was especially quiet, and I wondered what they were thinking when a hand went up. It was little Willie who said, "Mrs. Heddens, we are all beautiful in our own way."

Through twenty-nine years of teaching special students, I have considered myself blessed by the privilege. At age nine, I knew I wanted to be a teacher. I was just an average student back then, so I wasn't sure that was possible. As I matured, I became a better student and was able to go to college to become a teacher. Through it all, I never considered being a special education teacher. In fact, special education didn't really exist until after I had finished my bachelor's degree. If I hadn't given birth to a child with Down syndrome, that idea would probably have never occurred to me. But God had a plan for me, and that has made all the difference. What seemed like the greatest tragedy of my life, having a child with a disability, turned out to be my greatest blessing.

I like to say that I have the best students and the best parents. My students appreciate what I do for them, and they tell me so. When what I ask them to do is difficult, I tell them not to worry. It is my responsibility to make it possible for them to succeed. All I ask of them is to try. We are a team and work together. Any student in my class will help another student who is struggling. We are all teachers, and we are all students.

While my students respect me as their teacher, they also know me as their friend. I make it a point to spend some time each day talking with them individually, getting to know what is going on in their lives and what interests them. They invite me to their birthday parties, graduation parties, and even their weddings. I go if I can and always enjoy their company. I am the only one who has ever had my job. The position was created in 1983, when I was hired, and I've been there ever since. My students know I plan to retire in 2013, and they are already wondering who will take my place. Hopefully it will be someone who believes in them as much as I do, who is enthusiastic about teaching, and someone with a very big heart to hold all their love.

KIRSTIN'S SIDE OF THE STORY

I am proud of my mom for being a teacher. I am always proud of her and all the things she has accomplished. She cares about her students and helps them learn.

My fiancé, David, was one of her first students. He was Candra's boyfriend when they were in high school. I was only eight years old then. He was too old for me then, but now he is not.

Chapter Seven
℘☙
The Not Too Easy Reader

Friends have asked me how Kirstin learned to read. I tell them she learned in school like everyone else, but there really is more to the story. Some of the ladies at our church wanted to give the credit to Kirstin's Sunday school teacher. All of a sudden, it seemed that Kirstin was able to read the little Sunday school books. Kirstin's teacher, Mrs. Mobley, was somewhat upset with this version of the story, and rightly so, as she had been working with Kirstin for two years. Of course Mrs. Mobley deserves the credit. She had a wonderful reading program called Edmark and all the faith in the world that her students could learn to read.

Much of the credit also goes to Kirstin herself. I like to tell people that Kirstin learned to read by shear force of will. As her skills improved, she read every word she saw. This meant that she read all of the credits at the end of a movie or television program. If we ate in a restaurant, Kirstin had to read the entire menu. Once again we found ourselves being held hostage in restaurants. Kirstin read signs, billboards, and posters. She read and read until she could read almost anything.

As a young child, Kirstin loved books and wanted them read to her; her favorites she wanted read over and over. She inherited her brother's preschool books and nearly wore them out. I made sure she belonged to some kind of a book club, so there was always a fresh supply of fun things to read with her. She had some books on cassette tapes and took a cassette player with her everywhere, even on her bike. She wore out several tape players. She loved the Disney princesses books with the accompanying cassettes.

Kirstin liked to personalize her books; that is, she wrote or drew in them. This caused some problems with the library. They really don't have a sense of humor about such things, even when I was prepared to purchase the autographed copy. I recently donated her childhood books, but first I went through them to make sure they were in good shape. Kirstin liked to underline, especially names, and write in the margins. Many of the books were illustrated by Kirstin.

Reading has been an important part of my life since I was a young child. Now that I had a daughter who loved reading, I wanted to share my favorites with her. I enjoyed *Beezus and Ramona* and all of the Judy Bloom books. *Doctor Doolittle* was also one of my favorites. Kirstin wanted nothing to do with my suggestions. Instead, she discovered her favorites on her own. Her ultimate love was *The Baby-Sitter's Club*. One after another, she read them as fast as they were being published. The characters in *The Baby-Sitter's Club* became real people in our household. Kirstin told us about them in great detail. One day I noticed Kirstin doing something sneaky, so I thought I had better check it out. On one of the pages of a *Baby-Sitter's Club* book there was an advertisement for babysitting services, complete with the phone numbers of the club members. Kirstin was on the phone, trying to contact someone in the club.

Kirstin knew all about *The Baby-Sitter's Club,* for example when the books were first published (1986). Kirstin was eleven at the time and really getting into reading. They lived in Stoneybrook, Connecticut. We once went on a vacation to Connecticut and had a very difficult time convincing Kirstin there was no such place as Stoneybrook and that she couldn't drop by and visit her friends in the BSC.

Through Kirstin we met Mary Anne Spier, whose mother died when she was little, and Kristy Thomas, whose stepfather was a millionaire. Kirstin's favorite was Stacey McGill, so we heard the most about her.

Stacey had diabetes, which, I believe, Kirstin saw as a disability and so she identified with her. There was also Claudia Kishi, who was Japanese-American, very intelligent, and creative.

These were the people at our dinner table every night and in the car with us when we traveled. Kirstin never went anywhere without a *Baby-Sitter's Club* book, and we were right there at the bookstore to buy the next one when a new book came out. Besides the regular series, there were super specials, mysteries, and a portrait collection that consisted of autobiographies of the BSC members. Kirstin knew enough about the characters to write their biographies herself. New series were introduced, including *Friends Forever* and *Little Sister*. At one time we counted 116 BSC-related books in Kirstin's collection. Of course she had read them all, most of them more than once. Even today, Kirstin can tell you all about the characters and their lives in complete detail. I have a vague memory of the books I've read. Kirstin can still talk about the BSC as if she read the books yesterday.

In 1996, Ann Martin came to Prescott for a book signing. We took Kirstin and her friend Angela to the bookstore where it was being held. There was a very long line that encircled the building, and we waited for hours. Kirstin had difficulty finding a new book to buy for Ms. Martin to sign, because she already had most of them. Finally, it was her turn. Maybe it was my imagination, but it seemed that Ms. Martin spent a little more time talking to Kirstin than she did with the others. It is one of Kirstin's fondest memories.

Part of Kirstin's fascination with the BSC came from the fact that there were lots of kids with disabilities. There were kids in wheelchairs and kids who were deaf. When Dawn Schafer, one of the members added later, moved to California, she was hired to take care of a little girl with Down syndrome. All these special children were presented with dignity, and the babysitters enjoyed caring for them and doing things with them.

From *The Baby-Sitter's Club,* Kirstin moved on to *Sweet Valley High* and others. Of course she likes reading books that are a series, and she has to read them in order. But reading is a real passion. Kirstin will say, "Mom, I'm out of books." To her, it is the same as being out of food. Reading is her life.

Kirstin comes by this naturally. The members of our family are prolific readers. Christopher, my oldest grandchild, learned to read quickly and is a regular reader. Both of my granddaughters were impatient to learn to read. I recall Brenna, who was in kindergarten, saying, "I hope someone teaches me to read soon!" When Avery came along, she said almost the same thing. Avery claimed to be the best reader in the first grade. I'm not sure how she won the title, but I'm pretty sure it was deserved. Both of their parents are constantly reading. My mother tells me that my father, who died when I was young, never went anywhere without a book in his back pocket.

Kirstin's love of reading goes hand in hand with her love of writing. She wants to be an author someday, and maybe, with a little help, she will become one. She is forever writing stories about events from her daily life. The characters have the names of people she knows and likes, but the plots are purely made up. When she was in high school, the choir teacher overheard this conversation between Kirstin and her friend Adrianne.

> Adrianne: "Kirstin, you're going to get into a lot of trouble making up stories."
> Kirstin: "Adrianne, that's why they call it *fiction!*"

When Disney released the animated movie *Kiki's Delivery Service*, Kirstin wrote a letter to Disney to thank them for making a movie about her. She had already mailed the letter before I learned about it, but I always wondered if someone at Disney got a chuckle out of it. Why Kirstin decided this movie was about her is not totally clear. Maybe it's because the main character's name is Kiki or because Kirsten Dunst provides her voice. There is some physical resemblance, with Kirstin's short dark hair and almond eyes. Perhaps Kirstin identified with Kiki because they both have had to overcome a great deal to become confident, capable, young women.

Kirstin has always been in love with Disney characters. As a child, she watched the Disney Channel every day. Her favorite show was *Adventures in Wonderland*. From that show she gained so much helpful information about how to get along with others. One of the characters would have a problem, and in the course of the episode, they would work out their differences with the other characters. It was usually the queen who had the most problems. It was from the queen that Kirstin learned her favorite knock, knock joke. It went: Knock, Knock. Who's there? Queen. Queen who? Queen up your plate, or you don't get dessert. We heard that joke at dinner many times.

When Kirstin was in my class in high school, we produced a magazine. Kirstin's article was on one of her favorite topics: the Disney Channel. This is what she said:

> Ariel is pretty. Belle is gorgeous. *Kids Incorporated* is break dancing. *Adventures in Wonderland* is radical. I wonder about the Disney Channel. Happy anniversary, Disney Channel. *Avonlea* is beautiful. The Disney Channel is my favorite channel. The Disney Channel has my favorite shows.

Kirstin and I occasionally didn't see eye to eye when it came to Disney. When we went to see *Pocahontas*, I was upset about the inaccuracies in a historical event. In fact, I turned it into a writing assignment for my class. First I read a short biography of Pocahontas. Then we watched the movie. After that I read some other comments about the movie, including those from the Powatan people themselves. I asked my students to compare and contrast the events in the movie to the real-life story of Pocahontas. Kirstin, who was in my class at the time, could not find any differences between the real story and the movie.

Now that Kirstin has to earn a living, she is very frugal when it comes to buying books, which can be so expensive. There is a used bookstore next to the Safeway, where she occasionally shops for groceries. She can trade her used books for credit and then she can select books she wants to read. At first she resisted trading in her BSC books, but eventually she did. She accidentally traded in the book signed by Ann Martin but was fortunate enough to be able to buy it back before someone else did. I was surprised that her need to have new books outweighed her need to hold onto her beloved BSC, but I'm always surprised by Kirstin.

When my church library was being cleared out of older, less-popular materials, there was a huge amount of Christian romance novels up for grabs. I selected ten of them for Kirstin but asked Marge, who was in charge of the library, if I could have any books that no one took. A week later, she gave me a big box of books for Kirstin. It took her about a year, but she read every one, some of them twice.

On her last birthday, we gave Kirstin a Nook. She has had a membership card at Barnes and Noble for ten years at least, but she was never able to go there as often as she would have liked. Now she can browse and download books anytime she has "nothing to read." When we picked up the Nook at the store, it had to be set up, so the clerk there very patiently helped Kirstin, who had some trouble typing in what needed to be entered. Later, when I tried to connect her Nook to her wi-fi, I found that I had more trouble with the typing than she did. Her tiny fingers were much better suited to it than mine. Barnes and Noble offered a class where she could learn to use the Nook. Kirstin took that class and is having no trouble using it. Now that I have a Nook, I sometimes ask Kirstin for help with it. She shows me how to do things I didn't know my Nook could do. We are Nook friends. I recently loaned her *The Hunger Games,* which she enjoyed very much.

If I could give one gift to my students, it would be reading. I have had so many parents of adults with special needs tell me how much they wish their child could read. Those of us who have done it for most of our lives take reading for granted. But to someone who can't read, it means isolation from a part of our world. This is especially true in today's information age. My students want to be able to utilize the Internet, text their friends, or communicate on Facebook. All of these possibilities are closed when reading and writing are difficult or impossible. Fortunately, assistive technology has helped provide some pretty amazing equipment to allow access to all of these things. The downside is that it is expensive. While a high school student, the person might have access to the equipment, but after graduation, it is up to the family to provide it. In most cases, that is not possible.

Students who are not able to read recognize that they are different. I see them check out books they can't possibly read and carry them around. The books usually have bookmarks in them to give the impression that they are being read. It makes my heart ache when I can't do enough to help them. Students who don't read well are often good listeners, though, and they have amazing memories. That is how they compensate for not being able to read.

The workplace is another area where being able to read makes the difference between getting the job you want or settling for whatever job you can get. Even with Kirstin's job, she is sometimes required to study materials on a computer and then take a test. She has had to learn about forklifts—not how to use them, but how to stay out of their way. Another topic was the incinerator and what could and could not be thrown in it. Because Kirstin can read, she is able take the tests on her own. She was recently asked to take a test at work and was so pleased with herself when she scored 100 percent. Her boss can leave written instructions for her. Kirstin can read her employee handbook or information in her benefits packet. She knows when she is looking at junk mail or when it is something important she needs to deal with.

We just don't realize how much reading we do each day. Kirstin never needs help with a menu or finding movie times on the Internet. She can read her church missal or the weekly bulletin.

How much we take reading for granted came home to me through an experience with my mother-in-law, Mary. She was suffering from

Alzheimer's and forgetting many things. We had all gathered for Kirstin's birthday, and Kirstin was reading her cards out loud to everyone. Mary said, "She can do that." I knew what she meant: that Kirstin could read. What I hadn't realized was that Mary couldn't. The thought of that made me so sad that tears came to my eyes. Mary didn't really know our names anymore, or even where she was for that matter. But somehow the fact that she could no longer read made me feel especially sad.

I'm always amazed at how many of my students enjoy writing, even the ones who aren't very good readers. I have my students write in a journal. With today's technology, we do it on a laptop called a NEO. Each student has a NEO at his or her desk. My students send their writing to my computer through NEO Share. A special receiver allows my computer to talk to the NEOs. I can respond to what they write and my students can retrieve my messages on their NEOs. This helps me learn a little about them, and it gives them an incentive to read in order to find out what I said to them.

I cover my walls with posters, and I have an information board—anything I can think of to provide opportunities for them to read. Students in my classes have varying levels of reading abilities. Many of my students are very good readers. Some can read any words but have difficulty comprehending what they read. Other students have a lower independent reading level, which makes it difficult to read many of our classroom materials. We have to adapt what is done in the classroom to accommodate those students who don't read well. Still, it is difficult to get around to everyone, and they soon learn that being able to read means being more independent.

It is amazing the lengths some of my students will go to in order to learn to read better. I have had students walk miles to the public library to get tutoring assistance from the adult literacy program. Some students continue to avail themselves of those services after high school. I try my best to make sure everyone can read at least fourth-grade material. In that way, they are able to read newspapers, menus, and most of the things they will come in contact with as adults. Students who leave with a reading level lower than that may end up losing the ability to read because it is such a struggle. That's why I do my best to help them reach the highest level possible as long as they are in my class.

For most of my students, they are able to increase their reading skills by three or four grade levels during the four years they are with me, sometimes even five or six grade levels. I have had a few times when this was not possible. In some cases, greater effort on the part of the student might have helped. While I would like to think that everyone can learn to read, I'm afraid that may not always be possible. Still, I operate under the belief that it is as long as my student is willing to try.

Just because reading may be difficult, learning to appreciate good literature doesn't have to be sacrificed. I love to introduce my students to great writers. We don't read a watered-down version that has been rewritten using a lower level vocabulary. We read the original as the author wrote it. My students enjoy stories like James Thurber's, "The Catbird Seat." John Steinbeck was my favorite author in high school, so I'm happy to have them read *The Pearl*. It's a simple story with a valuable lesson about how family is worth more than the biggest pearl in the world. We even read a little Shakespeare. As for poetry, the writings of Robert Frost and my personal favorite, Emily Dickenson, express some important truths that are certainly not lost on my students.

My students' interests are extensive. Fortunately, they are able to learn a great deal from television. They can tell me facts I don't know about weather and storms, volcanoes and earthquakes. They are students of history and learn so much by watching the History Channel. Still, some of them are limited because they cannot follow up their interests by further reading, as most of us do. It is always my dream that I can help them achieve reading independence.

I will be forever grateful to everyone who had a hand in helping Kirstin learn to read. Her world has been expanded so much, because she is able to experience through books what she would never be able to experience in real life. There are no limits on her enjoyment possibilities. Even this project we are working on together has brought her pleasure because she has been able to read it for herself. As I have handed her chapter after chapter, she has eagerly turned the pages, reliving events she remembers and discovering who she is in her mother's eyes.

KIRSTIN'S SIDE OF THE STORY

I read every day. I like to read books that are exciting or funny. I like to read love stories because I'm in love with David. I do read history, romance, scary books, and mysteries. The characters in the stories make mistakes and learn from their mistakes. I learn from their mistakes too.

I don't read The Baby-Sitter's Club books anymore, but I still remember them. Claudia Kishi, one of the characters, likes junk food. Dawn Shafer is a health nut. Jessica Ramsey likes ballet. Mallory reads books about horses and dreams about them. Kristy Thomas's mouth always gets her into trouble. Mary Anne Spire gets very emotional like I do. She hardly knew her mother because she passed away when Mary Anne was born. Stacey McGill's parents worry about her all the time because of her diabetes. Abby is the newest member; she has asthma.

I like the babysitters because they have problems, but they don't let that stop them. The kids they babysit for have disabilities. Matt is deaf. There is a girl in a wheelchair. Charlotte Johnson is helped by Stacey to overcome her shyness. Dawn Shafer helps a little girl named Whitney, who has Down syndrome.

Now I read books for adults. I like Nora Roberts's books. Right now I'm reading Rilla of Ingleside. It is number eight in the Anne of Green Gables series. Rilla is Anne's daughter. She kind of looks like me because she has brown hair and hazel eyes. I have all of the Avonlea books on my Nook.

If I couldn't read, my life would be boring. I would not have been able to read The Baby-Sitter's Club or the Avonlea books. I have to do some reading at work and in church. If I couldn't read, I wouldn't be as independent, because someone would have to help me. I have been able to read Facebook and Livemail, so I know what my friends are doing. I sent my boss a music video on Facebook. I had to read to figure it out by myself. My mom said she doesn't know how to do that, but I can because I can read.

If someone is having trouble learning to read, I would tell them not to give up. You can do it if you put your mind to it. Read as much as you can and you'll get better at it. We all have problems. Yours is learning to read, but you can solve it. Find a good teacher who will help you and never give up on you.

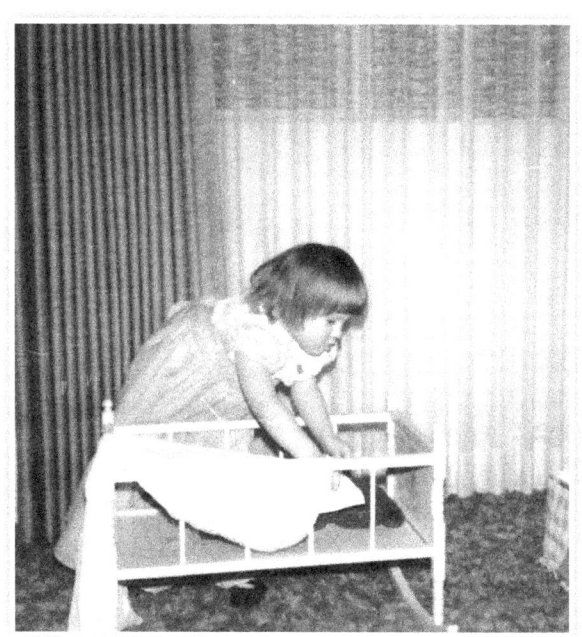

Kirstin age 2: "I'm the Mama"

Kirstin age 3: Promotion to regular preschool

This Little Light of Mine

Crusin' on her bike at age 4

Dressed as Rainbow Bright

Dancing with Dad

Two American girls: Kirstin Heddens and Kirsten Larsen

Kirstin meets her favorite author, Anne Martin

Look Mom! I won the car!

This Little Light of Mine

Kirstin and David at the Mardi Gras Prom

Working Girl

Chapter Eight

ಎಲ್ಲಾ

On to Higher Learning

After Kirstin completed three years at Heritage Middle School, we decided to try something different and took Chino Valley Unified School District up on its offer to tuition her to my high school. We had forged the way for those students coming up behind her, and once the dam broke, a wave of special needs students flooded into the middle school. Chino had no choice but to provide an appropriate program at that level. Now we were looking at having to do the same thing as Kirstin moved on to high school. After a little research, we did discover that there was one student in the self-contained program at Chino Valley High School. She was being taught in a closet. Actually, it was a small room off the library. She never left the room all day, even eating her lunch there.

We became the whistle-blowers, and our friend, who was the president of the school board, looked into the matter. When she discovered that it was true, she put an end to it. Since then, Chino Valley High School has developed an excellent program, focusing on both academic and functional skills. At the time Kirstin was preparing to go to high school, we wanted more for her than Chino could provide during her last four years of public education. I had worked very hard to develop my program. Why shouldn't my own daughter benefit from all of my hard work?

Kirstin was enrolled at Bradshaw Mountain High School for the fall semester of 1992. She was then seventeen years old, a few years older than the other freshmen. But because of her size, no one really noticed. That year, Kirstin was in the self-contained program and in regular PE. Fortunately, at the time we had split my program between me and another teacher, so Kirstin was not in my class all day. That first year, I had Kirstin for English and science only.

Transition to high school was a little challenging for Kirstin, but she soon adapted. There were some problems with the students in her PE class, but we were able to resolve those. Her bad habits from middle school sometimes got her in trouble, but overall, she was starting to mature and take responsibility for learning. Kirstin entered high school reading at about the fourth-grade level. Her best skills were in writing and her worst subject was math. The speech therapist continued to work with her on articulation, as her expressive and receptive language skills were already beyond what would be expected of someone with Kirstin's cognitive ability. By this time, Kirstin had braces on her teeth. Her palate had been spread twice, and that made more room for her tongue. She had a more natural appearance without her tongue always slightly protruding and more room to make her speech sounds.

The first challenge I had as Kirstin's teacher came shortly after school started. In English class, I assigned a writing activity. I showed my students the pencil sharpener and asked them to write a description of it. Everyone started to work on their writing assignment. Kirstin, however, made it quite clear that she had no interest in writing about the pencil sharpener. She had another topic in mind. I never said a word to her about what she was doing and made no effort to check on her writing. I continued around the room, looking over shoulders and making comments to the other students. When time was up, I called on various students to read their descriptions. After several had read theirs, we discussed how the descriptions were alike and how they were different.

Kirstin remained quiet throughout the discussion, but when we were finished, she asked if she could read her paragraph. I said that since she had chosen to write on a different subject, there was no reason for her to read it. She wasn't very happy with that answer and was even less happy when her paper was returned to her with a zero. I only had that problem once. From then on, whatever the writing assignment was, Kirstin stuck to the topic. I was never sure if that was the way she worked the teachers in the middle school or if she was testing me to see how things would go with her mom for the teacher. Either way, she found out how things operated in my classroom. I was really glad that was over with. Eventually, Kirstin blended in and was just like any other student in my class.

The mom/teacher line was blurred once again when a very serious situation occurred at our school. A distraught young man whose girlfriend had broken up with him brought a shotgun into the cafeteria. He climbed on a table and shot two holes in the ceiling. There were only a few students in the area at the time, and they were all safely removed. While the police were on their way, two teachers tried to talk the student down.

Meanwhile, my students and I were in our classroom, which shared a common wall with the cafeteria. The wall was lined with lockers, which I surmised would provide us with some protection, but I quickly moved the students into the kitchen area on the other side of the room. Huddled together there, I began to take inventory and soon realized there was a student missing. I had no idea where he was and became quite concerned. My aide didn't have any idea where he was either as we continued to hear gunshots.

The situation was eventually resolved without any injuries. The angry student was talked down and taken away by the police. It wasn't until the entire incident was over that I realized I was missing more than one student. Kirstin had gone to speech therapy earlier and had not been with us. It seemed strange that I hadn't noticed she was missing, but I guess I knew somehow that she would be safe.

Kirstin's progress in high school was, to say the least, amazing. By the time she graduated, she was able to read and comprehend high school level material. Her writing and spelling skills improved. Even math, which had always been her downfall, was beginning to make sense to her. I taught the higher-level math class, and by her junior year, she was in my class. Kirstin was able to work with fractions and large numbers. We tried her on some geometry and even algebra. It took her a little longer to grasp the concepts, but as long as she could use her calculator, she was able to do anything we threw at her.

Even more astonishing than her academic progress was the fact that her next psychoeducational evaluation showed her IQ had jumped ten points. I asked the psychologist how that was possible, and he said that this was more accurate than the other tests, because she was better able to show what she could do. All of her academic and language skills were at that level or higher, confirming the IQ score. Well, so much for the plateau theory. Obviously Kirstin hadn't reached it yet.

The four years in high school were the most enjoyable years of Kirstin's education. She joined the choir in her sophomore year and found it to be a truly delightful experience. She loved her teacher, Ms. Lester, and the feeling seemed to be mutual. While Kirstin's singing ability is certainly below that of most students in choir, she was accepted by her peers and performed in all of their concerts. Sometimes it was difficult for her to remember all of the words to every song, but she always gave it her best.

A few years before Kirstin became a high school student, the student council bylaws had been amended to include a special education representative. A student from my class served as the first representative, but after that student graduated, Kirstin was elected to the position. At the beginning of school every year, the student council members went to a leadership conference, which involved an overnight trip. Kirstin was able to attend with them and had the opportunity to be on her own with her peers. This was a great experience for her and a chance for me to loosen the apron strings a little.

Kirstin attended the weekly student council meetings and took notes. Then she reported back to the special education classes. She was chosen as student council representative of the year by the student council sponsors. The reason, I was told, was that Kirstin was always prepared. She took notes during the meetings, and when it came time to vote, she knew exactly what she was going to do. She truly was a leader.

We looked for as many mainstreaming opportunities as we could for Kirstin. In the vocational department, there were a number of life skills classes we thought she could benefit from. First she took a cooking class, and later she enrolled in Independent Living. Kirstin was able to attend these classes on her own, without any help from an aide, and the teacher was very cooperative. Besides gaining some important skills, like maintaining a checkbook and handling finances, Kirstin was spending more of her day with her nondisabled peers. There she had friends, and some who were not so friendly, but she had to learn how to manage. Her senior year, she was moved into the resource classroom for English and had no problem keeping up with the students there.

Throughout her four years in high school, Kirstin longed to be the president of the GOALS Club. This was a club I started with my students that continues to this day. GOALS stands for Grab Opportunities and Learn Something. The purpose of the GOALS Club is to participate in school events, such as parades and carnivals and to serve our community by helping with recycling or collecting items for Operation Christmas Child. Every year, Kirstin was elected to an office. She was the secretary, treasurer, and the vice president. The only office she hadn't served in was the presidency. Finally, as a senior, she became the president. That year we built a float for the homecoming game and raised money for the Heritage Park Zoo by recycling aluminum cans. Kirstin was a good president, who led the meetings and kept everyone on task.

High school was a wonderful time for Kirstin, who loved learning and was gaining new skills every day. She participated in as many activities as she could. Every Friday in September and October, when there was a home football game, she would be there, cheering on the team. We always sat with Olga, the coach's wife, who was also Kirstin's boss in the cafeteria. When the cheerleaders yelled, "Freshmen, what's your number?" Kirstin would shout back proudly, "Ninety-six, ninety-six, ninety-six."

Kirstin was there for the homecoming game and attended the dance afterward. I have to chuckle a little when I think about her freshman year. She and her friend Adrianne went to the dance together. Craig and I were there as chaperons. We watched as Kirstin and Adrianne asked nearly every guy in the gym to dance. Over and over they were turned down. We were amazed at their persistence, and eventually it paid off. Two of the football players went over and asked them to dance. Their evening had been made.

As a sophomore, Kirstin was invited to the prom. Her date was a student in my class. Shopping for a prom dress was fun for both of us. I made an appointment for Kirstin to have her hair done, and she was gorgeous, even if I do say so. Before the dance, she and her date went out to dinner. Then they danced the night away with their fellow students.

It is a tradition at our high school to have dress-up days during spirit week, the week before homecoming. It was also a tradition for seniors to be auctioned off in a slave sale. We no longer have this event, but during Kirstin's senior year, she wanted to participate in the auction. She was purchased by some of her friends, who dressed her up as the New Year's Eve baby. She was a good sport about it and wore her costume (uh . . . diaper) over her clothes the entire day.

In the summers, Kirstin traveled with an organization called Horizon Tours. This was a vacation opportunity for teens and adults with special needs. Kirstin went on the California trip, which included all the major theme parks in one week. The trips were well supervised with an excellent adult-to-student ratio, but it was still another opportunity for Kirstin to exert some independence. She had to make decisions for herself and learn to get along with people from different backgrounds. This was not only a chance for Kirstin to grow but for me to learn to let go a little more.

High school was such a memorable experience for Kirstin, I think she would be happy to return to it. But like all good things, it was coming to an end. As she was completing the second semester of her senior year, panic was setting in with her parents. All these years I had been talking about the importance of planning for transition into adulthood. But now that my daughter was ready for it, I felt that I didn't really know anything about transition at all.

Kirstin graduated with her friends, wearing a cap and gown and walking across the stage with all the other graduates. She received a regular diploma for completing a course of study that, though modified, met all the graduation requirements. Following the ceremony, she attended the all-night party, while her parents went proudly home for some much-needed sleep.

All the time Kirstin was in high school, it had been her plan to go to college. This seemed like a good idea to us. It would give her a chance to gain some more skills and independence before starting a career. I had a friend who taught the English and math classes below the 101 level. She was confident that Kirstin would be able to have some success in those classes and encouraged me to enroll her. Yavapai Community College had its own entrance test, so she would not have to take the ACT or SAT. That was a relief. As predicted, Kirstin did not do well enough on the test to take any classes above the 100 level. She registered for reading, writing, math, and aerobics. Unfortunately, my friend had some health problems and would not be teaching any of the classes. We still had high hopes for Kirstin's success.

Kirstin qualified for tutoring, and I stood in line with her to sign up. (I didn't ask her if it was the boys' line or the girls' line.) While we were waiting, she expressed fear that she would not be able to use the clock to get to classes on time. In high school, there were bells, and there were classes one right after the other. She knew that college would be different, and her schedule left lots of open time between classes. Some classes met on Monday, Wednesday, and Friday, while others were Tuesday Thursday classes. As we stood there, Kirstin looked at the clock every few minutes and told me the time to the minute. At least our first college problem was solved.

Our next stop was the campus bookstore, where Kirstin had to purchase her books. Once that was accomplished, we took a tour of the campus, so she would know where to find everything. We followed her schedule to locate each classroom, the gym for her aerobics class, the library, the test-taking center, and the cafeteria. With that, Kirstin was as ready as she could be.

Kirstin started her classes with enthusiasm, but that soon waned. Some of her teachers seemed to think she did not belong there. I was amazed that a teacher who had only eight students was not able to give her any extra help, when I had twenty, and no one was neglected in my classes. Teachers' attitudes in college are apparently different from those of high school teachers. Where I saw it as my responsibility to make sure my students learned what they needed to know, college teachers put all of the responsibility on the students. Kirstin did her best to pay attention in class. She brought home the assignments, and I read the instructions. Then I helped her follow them according to what I thought the teacher was asking her to do. Still, it never seemed like she had things right.

Math was an even bigger problem for her. Kirstin was able to grasp most math concepts, but she relied heavily on her calculator. The lower-level math classes were teaching basic math, and students were not allowed to use a calculator. This resulted in some confrontations and rude comments from her teacher. Still, Kirstin hung in there and finished two semesters. She only had a few credits by the end of the year, and there was no question about going back. One year of college was all she needed to decide that it wasn't for her.

Kirstin continued to take water aerobics and other classes of interest. Later, when special needs classes were introduced, she enrolled in most of those. At different times, Yavapai College has tried to provide for the special needs population, but it has never been a major concern for the school. While it is called a community college, I believe they are overlooking a large section of the community who would benefit from and enjoy taking college classes.

At least one college has been able to tap into this previously ignored population. Some of my former students are attending Eastern New Mexico University in Roswell. Prior to enrolling, it was very exciting for the students and their parents to visit the school during spring break as other students do. The offerings at EMNU are geared toward the needs of students such as mine. They have the opportunity to experience dorm life that is more supervised than regular college dorms, while still providing them a chance to enjoy independence. They are able to choose training programs that include child-care attendant, refrigeration and air conditioning maintenance, and veterinarian technician assistant. The offerings are very similar to the types of career goals my students have, but training programs are not usually made accessible to them.

In addition to the occupational training, my students attend classes in independent living, physical education, CPR, and driver's education. Graduates of this program have excellent job prospects, as the school has a 75 percent employment rate for graduates from their special program. This unique opportunity is everything a parent of a special needs high-schooler could hope for.

Home during breaks, the college students drop by and visit. It is amazing how they have matured in such a short time. They are so excited to tell me about their lives and all that is going on in college. When they complete their programs, they will return to the community with certification in their chosen fields and a greater chance of getting a job, as well as the skills they need to live on their own.

I am amazed that more community colleges haven't caught on to the realization that there is such an unserviced and underserviced group of potential students. I suppose it is expensive to set up such a program, but considering the availability of students and potential funding through programs like Rehabilitative Services, such expenses could be justified. The mere title—community college—would suggest that college should be available to everyone in the community. That should include the special needs population. Perhaps with the success of the program in New Mexico and other such programs, more colleges will discover this potential for increasing their student numbers. As more people in our country strive for higher education, the need for trained people in maintenance, animal care, child care, and food service will be needed.

It seems like a perfect time to begin preparing an almost previously untapped supply of human resources.

In the spring of 1997, Kirstin's formal education came to an end with the completion of sixteen years in public school and one year of community college. Twenty-two years after the passage of Public Law 94-142, the law establishing special education for all students, we hoped that Kirstin had been adequately prepared for adult life. What her life would be like, we didn't yet know, but we did know that with Kirstin's determination and those skills she had acquired, there wouldn't be much to hold her back.

KIRSTIN'S SIDE OF THE STORY

I'm glad I could go to Bradshaw Mountain High School. It had the best program for me. I was happy to have my mom for a teacher. I think I was her teacher's pet. English was my best subject. I like reading and writing. I have a lot of good skills. Math was my worst subject. My mom taught me to do math. I love Miss Lester so much. She taught me to sing as best as she could. I was happy to be in student council back then. I did very well at it. I always liked cooking and independent living. I am very independent at a lot of things, like keeping my checkbook and finances. I liked going to the football games.

It was fun spending the night at my friends' houses or having them spend the night with me. We could stay up all night, listening to music and talking. Sometimes we went to dances together. I even went to the prom with Shawn Desjardin.

I wanted to go to college. The classes I took were hard. I had a tutor to help me with some of my classes. College is not like high school. I do realize that. Some of my teachers gave me a hard time. The worst was my math teacher. She jumped all over me and said nasty things to me. I didn't like it one bit. I had a rough time with my homework. Math was a big problem back then.

I have some advice for high school students who want to go to college. College is not an easy thing to do, but you can learn to do it. Do the best you can. That is all you can do. All you have to do is believe in yourself. Tell yourself that you are special in a lot of ways. It does not matter who you are as long as you have parents and friends to help you. Don't let any teachers tell you that you can't do it.

I did like the special needs classes I took with Jean McGuire at Yavapai College. We learned about other countries and how to cook. There was a class where we learned how to write notes and letters. The best classes were the singing classes, especially the ones where we studied Broadway musicals.

Chapter Nine

ഇരു

All the World's a Stage

In all the books I've read about Down syndrome, I have never seen anything about being dramatic, but I really believe that should be included in the description. Most of the people I know with Down syndrome are dramatic. They are animated, impish, and absolutely adorable actors and actresses. It is my theory that it is a trait carried on their extra chromosome, along with other traits such as being loving and cheerful. Kirstin has been a little actress all her life. When she was a preschooler, she would order french fries from the speaker on the car dashboard. At home one day, I came running as fast as I could when I heard her shrieking. What I found was Kirstin on a stool, holding a doll over the edge. Our cat was circling below, and Kirstin was in the process of rescuing the doll from the dangerous animal.

After Kirstin's year in kindergarten, we took a family trip to Hawaii. It was our summer vacation, but it was a little bit of a business trip for me as the Region Eight vice president for Jaycee Women. At the end of our vacation, there would be a meeting I was in charge of, but first we would have some fun. Kirstin is a great traveler and enjoys seeing new places. We have pictures of her on the trolley on Kauai, singing into her imaginary microphone.

It was at the Polynesian Cultural Center that Kirstin was really a star. We were making our way from island to island, around the exhibits, and at some of them, ladies were invited to come up and don grass skirts to try the traditional dances. I participated in the Hawaiian exhibit, and Kirstin wanted very badly to join me. She was unsuccessful that time, but when we reached the Samoan Island, there was no stopping her. Before I knew it, she was on the stage. They put a skirt on her that was nearly as big as she was and tied just under her armpits. As the music started, a group of Scandinavian tourists arrived. I wondered what they thought as this tiny girl in a huge skirt stomped up and down on the stage, pumping her arms and shaking her head. It was scary and funny all at the same time.

As I kicked off my meeting on Friday night, I asked my children to provide the entertainment. Michael had acquired a set of poi balls, two balls attached to cords. The balls are swung in circles and crossed over in a sort of juggling style. He had developed some skill with them and performed for my group of ladies. Kirstin followed his act with her version of the hula. By that time, she had her own grass skirt. Finally, they sang a song they learned on Kauai. As they sang, "I'm a palm tree, I'm a palm tree, I'm a palm tree through and through," they moved ever closer to their dad, who was seated on the edge of the stage. When they reached the end of the song, "But I'd rather be a palm tree than a coconut like you," they knuckled their dad on the head. It was adorably funny, and I was really impressed with both of my children.

Kirstin has been featured and photographed many times in news articles and publicity pamphlets. The highlight of her press exposure was when she was invited to make a commercial for Camp Fire Boys and Girls. The Arizona Cardinals was the new team in town, and they were asked to make a public service announcement for Camp Fire. Kirstin was chosen to participate in the commercial. She wore her uniform skirt and vest with all her emblems. The commercial was filmed in a park, and Kirstin went down the slide. At the end of the commercial, they all gathered around and said, "Go, Campfire Boys and Girls."

During her elementary and middle-school years, Kirstin had many opportunities to be before an audience. There were always choir concerts or a visiting musician who helped the students make instruments and provide an evening performance for their families. Kirstin never shied away from any of those opportunities; she was always front and center, doing her best.

Every year at church there was a Christmas pageant. Because of her size, Kirstin was always an angel. One year, however, she was chosen to play the part of Mary. There were no lines to learn, but she had to walk with Joseph as they tried to find a place to stay. Finally, they ended up at the manger, where Kirstin placed the baby Jesus in his bed. She took her role quite seriously and was a very convincing Mary.

Kirstin has a way of dropping "zingers" when you least expect them. One day when she was about eight years old, we were coming home from church, when I asked her what she had learned in Sunday school. Very dramatically she began, "Jesus took the bread and He broke the bread. He passed the bread to everyone at the table." I was really impressed with how well she was paying attention in class—until she continued, "And then He took the spaghetti sauce . . ."

On another occasion, Kirstin got the best of me again. Prescott Valley was a very small, rural town when we moved there. At the end of our road was a pond. Today it is beautiful twin lakes, surrounded by a park, but when we lived there, it was a dirty pond. Michael spent a lot of time fishing things out of the pond and filling Kirstin's little swimming pool with various creatures. He then used our encyclopedias to identify his catches.

One day Michael and one of his friends came rushing in from the pond to announce that there was a naked man there. It turned out that there was a man with some mental problems, who was taken away by the police after he had removed his clothing. Kirstin wasn't allowed to go down to the pond, but I thought it was important to prepare her in case she was outside and this man didn't remain in the pond area. "What would you do," I asked her, "if you saw a man with no clothes on?"

"I would come in the house right away and tell you or Dad."

"Good answer," I told her. "That is exactly what you should do."

Later, when Craig came home from work, I wanted Kirstin to show off a little. "Tell your dad what you would do if you saw a naked man," I insisted.

With a twinkle in her eye, Kirstin quipped, "I would say, 'Ooh, you're *naked!*'"

From her performances in gymnastics to choir performances and school and church pageants, Kirstin has not shown any embarrassment about being in the limelight. She is a natural. This is why I had no problem convincing her to accompany me when I was asked to give a presentation to the Chino Valley Lionesses Club. They sponsor a camp in Pinetop, Arizona. Kirstin and many of her friends attended the camp every summer. I was glad to come and speak at their meeting as a way of saying, "Thank you for your generosity." I was especially grateful, as the camp was free to all campers. We only had to provide Kirstin's transportation to and from the camp. I had a little video to show them and spoke about what a wonderful experience the camp is. It has a beautiful indoor pool and there are so many terrific, age-appropriate activities. But the person they really wanted to hear from was Kirstin, who stole the show. She had everyone's attention as she described her camping experience and how much fun she had at camp. I spent hours preparing what I was going to say, but Kirstin spoke from the heart.

In movies and television shows, I have seen many actors portray people with mental challenges, some well, some not so convincingly. What has always amused me is the fact that no actor can ever portray a person with Down syndrome except a person who has Down syndrome. And there I have seen some excellent acting.

I think, of course, of Corky on *Life Goes On*. The actor, Chris Burke, was nominated for a Golden Globe award for the role. I especially recall one episode where Corky was studying Edgar Allan Poe's "The Raven." The class was given a test on the poem. Corky and a girl in the class were accused of cheating. The girl claimed that Corky was copying from her test, but Corky insisted it was the other way around. To prove his innocence, Corky recited *The Raven* from memory. In filming the episode, Chris was going to be provided with cue cards, but he insisted on actually memorizing the poem. He said that if the audience was to believe it was possible for someone with Down syndrome to memorize a long poem like "The Raven," he needed to actually do it. One must admire his integrity as well as his acting ability.

When Kirstin was a senior in high school, an amazing opportunity came her way. I was at our parent-teacher conference, where the teachers were seated arena style around the cafeteria. Seated next to me was the drama teacher, Mrs. Fain, and we were both waiting for parents when she started telling me about a problem she had. She was in the process of producing three one-act plays staring senior students. One of the actors had received an F on his report card and was not eligible to be in the play. There were only three weeks left, and she needed to replace him. The problem was the role was for a child, so she needed someone small to play the part. She asked me if I knew anyone who might be able to take the role.

Before I had time to fully think about what I was getting her into, I immediately suggested Kirstin. Mrs. Fain asked me to bring her to the rehearsal the next day, and she would have her read. Of course, Kirstin was all excited about it, and so was I, although a little apprehensive.

Kirstin did very well at the reading, so she left with the script to a one-act play called *A Thing of Beauty*. It was about a man in the park with a piece of driftwood he found. He was enjoying it, placing it on the sidewalk and the grass to see how it looked. A policeman came along and told him to move it, or he would have to pay a fine. Next, a businessman came along, and he told the man with the driftwood that he needed to create an image if he wanted to sell the driftwood. Then a woman came along with her dog. She was only interested in the driftwood when she thought it was an expensive piece of art. No one appreciated the natural beauty of the wood until a little girl with a butterfly net came on the scene. She immediately recognized the wood as something special and wanted to hold it. Things were going fine, until her mother came after her and scolded her for talking to a stranger. Then the mother threw the wood away. After everyone left, the policeman came back and rescued the wood from the trash can.

Kirstin seemed like a natural for the part, but she would have lots of lines to memorize and a very short time in which to learn them. Our thirty-minute commute to school and back each day gave us time to practice her lines. Getting them all down in time for the performance seemed like an impossibility. "What have I gotten us into?" I asked Craig. "I don't think Kirstin can do it."

Of course I was wrong. A week before the performance, I heard Mrs. Fain speaking to the cast: "You should all know your lines by now. Look at Kirstin. She's only been with us for two weeks, and she already knows her lines. What is wrong with the rest of you?"

Kirstin was ready by the dress rehearsal, and for three nights, she turned in a beautiful performance. Once again, Kirstin came through when the task seemed impossible.

Singing in the choir is part of the curriculum in elementary school, but in high school, it is an elective. Kirstin chose to sing in the choir throughout high school. She enjoyed this very much and especially liked performing before an audience. She never had a solo but did sing as a member of a small group. Kirstin loved her choir teacher and had many friends in the choir.

Our local community college offered some classes for adults with special needs, and Kirstin enrolled in nearly all of them. They were taught by her very dear friend, Jean McGuire. One of the classes was a singing class. Jean taught them a variety of popular songs, and she accompanied them on the piano. Every Christmas there was a performance. This was a big event that Kirstin and her fellow students looked forward to with great anticipation.

While the singing was not what you would call professional quality, what they lacked in singing ability they made up for in enthusiasm. Kirstin invited her coworkers from the Costco bakery, and I was impressed that many of them came. I was even more impressed when they returned the following year.

Some of the singers were chosen for duets or solos, and twice Kirstin had that honor. Her singing ability has always been more appropriate for the shower, but on those occasions when she was given the assignment of singing a solo, her talents seemed to miraculously improve. The first year she sang, "I'll Be Home for Christmas," which she performed beautifully and with confidence. Her greatest singing accomplishment came the last year the class was offered. Kirstin was chosen to sing "It Came upon a Midnight Clear." This grand finale for the class was held at the Ruth Street Auditorium, a large facility. There on the huge stage was Kirstin at the microphone and Jean at the piano. Her voice rang out across the auditorium, and she sang every word with clarity. When she finished, she walked over to Jean and whispered something. Then she returned to the microphone. "I'm going to sing it again," she said to the audience. And she did as beautifully the second time as the first. I'll never forget the final words of the song: "To hear the angels sing." *Yes we did,* I said to myself, twice.

The college classes are no longer offered, but Kirstin and many of her friends moved on to another musical endeavor. That is, they play in a chimes choir at a local Lutheran church. They are called the Heavenly Chimers, a name the musicians came up with themselves. The group is made up of people with special needs, and they have a wonderful director named Jim. He has developed a numbering system that allows the chimers to make beautiful music. The chimes are really long tuning forks with a tapper that hits the tuning fork and makes it vibrate. The Heavenly Chimers perform at churches and in nursing homes. Listening and watching them is certainly a treat. Most of them play two chimes, sometimes even three. One day they were shorthanded, and I was called on to fill in. They make it look so easy, but I continually messed up, playing the wrong chime or playing at the wrong time. It is no surprise I haven't been asked to perform that duty again. Every Christmas, they perform their Christmas repertoire at several nursing homes. This is enjoyed by the residents and their caregivers.

Prescott Parks and Recreation's SNAP (special needs activities program) has a signing class that learns sign language for many popular songs. The performers use sign language to express the words to the songs in a flowing, rhythmic way. They perform at sports events and for the residents in many nursing homes. The expressions on their faces show pure joy at what they are doing. And the expression on the faces of the people in the nursing homes shows their appreciation and delight. Following the performance, the signers visit with the residents, bringing even more joy to their lives. Kirstin joined the signing class when it was first formed and participated in it for many years. She retired from the group about a year ago due to concerns with her shoulder joints.

While Kirstin was part of the group, they were invited to perform with Red Grammer, an award-winning singer and songwriter. He records songs that teach important values to children. All dressed in black, the SNAP signers were an awesome presence on the stage, signing as Red Grammer sang their favorite song, "Over the Rainbow." Then the signers accompanied Red Grammer as he sang his song, "See Me Beautiful"—a song with an appropriate message coming from the special signers.

Kirstin and her friends have always had a fascination with *The Wizard of Oz*. I'm not really sure why, but they try to include it in as many performances as they can. At a convention, they all dressed up in costumes and acted out a scene. Kirstin was Dorothy, because she has the costume, but there was a Cowardly Lion, Tin Man, and Scarecrow, not to mention the evil witch and Glinda, the good witch. It was entertainment at its best. Kirstin has a very special reason to love *The Wizard of Oz*. She was wearing her Dorothy costume at the Halloween dance when she met her fiancé, David.

It took Jim quite a while to find music for "Over the Rainbow" for the chimes choir, but he did manage to find it. After he adapted it for the Heavenly Chimers, they learned to play it beautifully. There are so many different notes in that song, it is truly amazing that they are able to hit each one perfectly.

Through the SNAP program, there is a dance each month. Kirstin and her friends look forward to these with great anticipation and preparation. There is always a theme, and they are always encouraged to dress up. Besides the usual Halloween, Christmas, Valentines' Day, and

St. Patrick's Day, there is also an Elvis night, tribute to the Beatles, a luau, and many others. There is even Mardi Gras Prom. No one is ever too old to dress up and have fun at the dances—parents and caregivers included. Dr. Spin is the DJ. He is in a wheelchair. Dr. Spin knows what kind of music the group enjoys but encourages the participants to bring in music. They never get tired of the macarena, the bunny hop, and YMCA.

Kirstin is always eager to participate in karaoke nights. She has been to some with her friends at Costco and goes prepared to sing her heart out. I, on the other hand, would never participate in a karaoke night except with Kirstin's special needs friends. With them, I feel comfortable singing or even belting out a tune, though a little off-key. No one judges, and no one cares. Everyone just has fun. I love the way they can relax and be themselves.

Most teachers would admit to being part performer. Certainly it helps when we are called on to compete with the elaborate electronic entertainment our students enjoy on a daily basis. Still, most entertainers would relish the thought of a captive audience guaranteed to applaud their efforts and not be judgmental when they bomb. This is part of what has kept me going for the past twenty-nine years. There is always someone to laugh at my meager attempts at humor.

Apart from the usual histrionics you expect to see demonstrated by teens, many of my students seem to truly enjoy drama. Every Monday, I enlist the aid of my students to teach the five new vocabulary words we are studying that week. Their favorite way to do this is to act them out. One group is assigned as guessers, and they have to be familiar with all five words in order to figure out which word is being portrayed. Sometimes they are required to do the acting without speaking; at other times, they are allowed to speak. I have other ways to introduce new words, but my students always request acting them out. Sometimes we reminisce about students who have graduated and the funny skits they put together.

If we are reading plays in a literature unit, I never have to beg for volunteers to read the parts. Even students who are not particularly strong readers want to take a role. On other occasions, I have asked my students to dramatize a story we have read, such as Hawthorne's "Doctor Heidegger's Experiment." It is always fun to see what they come up with and how different groups of students portray the same story in different ways.

Kirstin was in my class when we wrote a play titled *Paradise Motel*. It had some unseemly characters, such as Sly and Poopsy Otis; their daughter, Lulu; and Cordenia Loveless, their maid. Through the course of the play, it becomes obvious that something shady is going on in the back room of the motel, and the FBI is onto it. The owners of the motel are warned by their town's mayor, Meek Evans. (My students wanted to name him after a very colorful Arizona governor, but I thought that was inappropriate. Meek Evans was our compromise.) Three guests come to the motel: a businessman, Weldon Rumproast; a shady lady named Sadie LaRue; and a seeker of lost souls, Jessica Pulpit. Two of my students wanted to be police, so we have two officers—Casey and Tracy—on the scene to make arrests. There is also a moonlighting tooth fairy. (It's a low-budget production so we couldn't afford a real fairy godmother.)

By the end of the play, Sly, Poopsy, and the mayor are caught with counterfeit money by the FBI agent who turns out to be their daughter, Lulu. Weldon and Cordenia are married—by the moonlighting tooth fairy, of course.

In my classroom over the years, I have had some talented performers. Several of my students have been members of the men's or women's high school chorus. Most of them just blend in with the rest of the choir, and there is nothing wrong with that. However, some of them truly stand out and are given solos or lead parts. I have students who are great dancers and who design their own choreography. There is a young man in my class who can do impressions of our class—all of the students, aides, and the teacher. His act is hilarious, and his impersonations are amazingly accurate. It might be difficult for him to concentrate in class, but I can only imagine the powers of observation needed to catch our nuances and idiosyncrasies the way that he does.

We have many personas, faces we put on depending on where we are and who we are with. It is easy to lose sight of who we really are. Kirstin and others like her only know how to be themselves. While it seems like they are natural actors, the truth is they are just acting naturally. They are the real deal. Their emotions are genuine, from the heart. Because they are who they appear to be, they assume everyone else is as well. They do not judge or look for hidden agendas. That is why it is so easy to relax and be oneself with them. When I am fortunate enough to be able to spend some time with Kirstin and her friends, I can let down the barriers and, for a time, not worry about what others think. It is more refreshing than a day at a spa.

KIRSTIN'S SIDE OF THE STORY

I loved being in the high school choir. I miss Miss Lester and my friends from high school. I do like to act, and I had fun being in the play. My favorite line was, "Ah Mom!" Everyone treated me like a part of the cast. When the play ended, we had a party. I really miss the classes Jean McGuire taught, especially the singing classes. I liked performing on stage for my friends at Costco.

Now I'm in the chimes choir. I usually play the four and three. Sometimes I also play a black nine. The black chimes are sharps. We play from big sheets. The notes are numbered 1-19. The chords are in a line. Jim calls it an ice cream cone. When I play a quarter note, I have to damp it on my chest. The hardest songs we play are "It's a Small World" and "Over the Rainbow," because they have so many different notes.

My mom wants to know why we like The Wizard of Oz so much. I think it is because everyone in the story has problems, but they have what they need to solve their problems. The Scarecrow wishes for a brain. He thinks he isn't smart, but he really is. Tin Man wishes for a heart. The Wizard tells him, "A heart is not judged by how much you love, but by how much you are loved by others." The Cowardly Lion wishes for courage. He faces the Wicked Witch, and he is brave when he needs to be. Dorothy wants to go home. Glinda tells her she always has the power to go back home. The ruby slippers help her when she says, "There's no place like home." Everyone is wishing for something, but they have it all the time. They just don't realize it until the Wizard points it out.

I love karaoke. I have my own karaoke machine. I sing and dance on my days off. I like Disney, country western, and rock. At the dances, David and I always dance up a storm. David brings a CD or two. I used to think I wanted to be a country western rock star. Now I'm happy being a worker at Costco and singing and dancing just for fun.

Chapter Ten

ஐ ௸

Working Girl

It's five o'clock in the morning. I roll over in bed and remember that I am alone. Fifteen minutes later, Craig lies down next to me, fully clothed. He has just returned from the forty-five-minute round-trip he makes each morning to take Kirstin to work. Her job in the bakery at Costco begins at 5 a.m. five days a week. Each morning, Craig and Kirstin are up at 3:45, and by 4:30, they are on the road. This was our routine for the first six months that Kirstin worked at Costco. It was a miracle that she got that job in the first place. We weren't about to mess it up.

Kirstin's year in college bought us some time, but now we had to think about what would come next. We all agreed that Kirstin needed a job. I worked with many of the coordinators at Rehabilitative Services, so that seemed like the best place to start. Once Kirstin qualified for their services, she was sent for testing. It was a very comprehensive series of tests to determine her skills and work potential. The testing showed that she was capable of competitive employment.

For two years in high school, Kirstin had a job in the school cafeteria. She was a runner, which meant that when a student ordered food, Kirstin would go get it, while the person she worked with collected the money. Kirstin worked with Olga Moran, who requested her. Olga went to our church, so she had known Kirstin since she was a tiny girl. Olga told me that Kirstin was the best runner, because she paid attention to what the students ordered. Then she immediately went to get the food. Other runners waited until the cafeteria worker told them what to get. When Olga turned around to tell Kirstin what to get, the food was already at her elbow.

After Kirstin graduated from high school, Olga was promoted to cafeteria manager of an elementary school. She wanted Kirstin to come to work with her, but the district food service director wasn't willing to take a chance on a special education student. Years later, he did take such a chance on another student, who was able to go to work for Olga after high school.

Besides the cafeteria job, Kirstin was able to get some additional work experience one summer through a program called the Job Training Partnership Act (JTPA). The purpose of JTPA was to give opportunities to students from low-income families and those in special education. To be in the program, Kirstin had to first get a job. These were jobs specifically developed by JTPA, and she was given a list of places where she could apply. Kirstin had to call and make an appointment for an interview, prepare an application, and compete with other students for the jobs. There were not enough jobs to go around, so some students wouldn't make it in.

One of the places Kirstin applied was the Chino Valley Library. The librarian at the time was Mr. Rothlisberg. Saying his name was very difficult for Kirstin, but she practiced over and over. It was fun to listen in as she called the library and asked to speak to "Mr. Rawisburg." But Kirstin was determined and made all the calls herself. He eventually did grant her an interview but chose another applicant for the job.

Kirstin continued to work her way down the list of job possibilities until they were almost exhausted. Then she called the Arizona Joint Labor Training Center. It was in a remote area north of Chino, but I drove her out there for an interview. The manager talked with her for a while and then said, "Why not? Let's give her a chance." Kirstin was hired with the awesome title of "commissary assistant."

Getting a job qualified Kirstin for a week of training with JTPA. She worked on filling out applications, interviewing skills, and workplace skills. After the training week, Kirstin started working as a commissary assistant. That meant she helped prepare food for the workers at the training center. She worked hard there for eight hours a day, five days a week for six weeks of the summer. She was paid minimum wage and earned about $1,000. That was the first year Kirstin had to file a tax return.

At least Kirstin had some work experience to put on her résumé. Now with Rehabilitative Services on board, she was ready to get a job. First they sent her to Yavapai Exceptional Industries (YEI) for an authentic work evaluation. The purpose of this was to see how Kirstin would perform in a work setting. When she was in high school, I had to visit YEI to talk about a student of mine who was working there. Kirstin was with me, and I suggested she might want to come in and see what the place was like. She said she was not interested and wouldn't even get out of the car. Working at YEI was now acceptable, because it was a means to an end.

A few months after enrolling with Rehabilitative Services, Kirstin was hired to work at the Taco Bell in Chino. She worked four hours a day, five days a week, and was paid minimum wage—$5.75 an hour. Her job was maintenance, which meant that she wiped down tables, scrubbed the table legs, emptied the trash, and filled the napkin and straw dispensers. Kirstin was a hard worker and hustled for the entire four hours.

The other workers at Taco Bell were teenagers. Even the area manager, who traveled to all of the Taco Bells in the area, was in her early twenties. Kirstin didn't make any friends among her coworkers, and they did nothing to make her job easier or more fun. In fact, when Kirstin struggled to remove the trash bags from the trash cans, it was customers who lent her a hand.

One day when I went to pick Kirstin up from work, she had been asked to remain for a meeting. The area manager wanted to talk to the workers about customer service. Apparently some of them had been messing around at the drive-thru window, and customers were complaining. As she talked, I noticed two of the workers blowing the papers off of straws at each other. "Well," I said to Kirstin after the meeting, "she sure has a handle on things."

So Kirstin's first job wasn't that great, but we all had jobs like that when we were starting out. It is part of our life experiences and contributes to who we are. So Kirstin had her first job and learned a little bit about herself and what she is capable of. She also learned about workplaces and how to get along. She did her job even when working conditions weren't ideal. She did it without complaint and without expecting compliments or recognition. While she worked at Taco Bell, she had Linda Smith, a job coach, to help her with any difficulties. Linda checked in with Kirstin from time to time. She was aware of the working conditions at Taco Bell and knew Kirstin was handling it as well as could be expected. Linda was very supportive and helpful.

Taco Bell cut Kirstin's hours to two hours per day but still expected the same amount of work from her. It was obvious that she needed to find a different job. At the same time, Craig had struck up a friendship with the general manager of Costco. They both had an interest in hunting and did some together. Craig started talking to him about a job for Kirstin. The general manager wanted to think about it for a few days. At a meeting of the department managers, he asked if anyone would be willing to take on an employee like Kirstin. Donna Rogers, the manager in the bakery, had a son at our high school. She wanted to give Kirstin a chance.

Kirstin was asked to fill out a job application and address it to the attention of the general manager. The application was fast-tracked, and the next thing we knew, she was going for an interview. Linda Smith accompanied her there, and she was hired on the spot. On her birthday, June 9, 1999, Kirstin went to her orientation as a brand-new employee of Costco.

After the orientation, I helped Kirstin fill out her employee paperwork. I was looking through her packet when I came to the sheet that explained about her pay rate and benefits. A sick feeling came over me when I saw that she would be paid $8 an hour. I couldn't imagine how Kirstin was going to be able to do any job worth $8 an hour and was sure that she would not have this job very long. I didn't say anything to her about my fears, but it was difficult to shake the thought that she might be fired.

Just like she did at Taco Bell, Linda Smith helped Kirstin through her first few weeks as her job coach. Linda came in and watched Kirstin perform her tasks and offered suggestions for doing them faster. After a month on the job, Linda only showed up occasionally to see if there were any problems. By the time Kirstin had been working a year, Rehabilitative Services closed her file and marked her as a success.

Working four hours entitled Kirstin to one fifteen-minute break. She had no problem with stamina, and the break was sufficient. Her only problem was knowing when to come back from break. If her break was at 8:00, she knew she needed to be back at 8:15, but what if she left for break at 8:07 or 8:12? Then she was not sure what time it would be fifteen minutes later. I was able to help her solve that problem by getting her an organizer that had a clock and a calculator. She could look at the clock and then add fifteen minutes to the time. That way she knew exactly what time to be back. Kirstin only needed the organizer for a few months. By then she was able to add and subtract minutes in her head.

Math was never Kirstin's best subject, but when she needs it, she seems to be able to do it. Working in the bakery required some math. There were a certain number of cookies or bagels in each box, a certain number fit on the baking sheets, and a certain number of baking sheets fit on a rack. Every day, Kirstin would look at her assignment to see how many boxes she needed to do. Then she would calculate how many baking sheets and how many racks she needed. That was lots of math, but she was doing it in her head.

For the first three months, Kirstin was on probation. Like most companies, Costco had standards of performance that had to be met. Kirstin's work in the bakery consisted of arranging cookies and bagels on baking sheets and then putting them on racks so they were ready to bake. She was expected to do thirteen boxes in the four hours she worked there.

After Kirstin had been working in the bakery for two months, Craig talked to the general manager to find out how she was doing. He said that she was not fast enough to meet the standard. They had decided to extend her probation period to 120 days, but he doubted that she would make it. He said after that they would try her on some other jobs, such as folding clothes. If she couldn't meet the standard there, they would have to let her go. It seemed that my worst nightmare was coming true.

I guess I forgot that this was Kirstin we were talking about. By the time she finished the first ninety days, she was meeting the standard and was off probation. She had made it over the first hurdle. At her first-year anniversary, she was evaluated again. She had lots of room for improvement but was doing well enough to continue. She was given a raise to $10 an hour, but along with that came a new standard, sixteen boxes. This was a real challenge, but Kirstin was able to reach that, too.

Working in the bakery was hard work, but it was also fun. Kirstin's coworkers accepted her as one of them from the start. They invited her to baby showers and going-away parties. They told her about their lives and their problems. Kirstin even went to a Country Thunder concert in Phoenix with Donna Rogers and another coworker.

Even though Kirstin seemed to be doing well at work, in the back of my mind was still the thought that she might lose her job. Donna Rogers was transferred to Kansas City, and that meant Kirstin would have a new manager. This, of course, brought new fears. In fact, she worked for several temporary managers until there was a permanent one. Each manager had different ideas about how things needed to be done, and Kirstin constantly had to adjust. She had one manager who would say, "There's no crying in the bakery."

My fears were finally put to rest when something very unexpected and somewhat traumatic happened. The health department inspectors were in the bakery, and everyone was concentrating on that. But Kirstin was going about her job as usual. She went to the sink to wash her hands, unaware that someone had moved a big Hobart mixer behind her. When she turned around, she fell into the mixing bowl and hurt her arm. She seemed to be just a little sore, but a few days later, while she was at work, her arm started hurting so badly she couldn't move it. My mom was called and told to take her to Prescott Valley Primary & Urgent Care Clinic.

Frustrated, my mom called me at work and asked me to come to the urgent care clinic. The problem was that Kirstin needed to fill out paperwork, and she couldn't lift her arm, let alone write. When I got there, she was cringing in pain, which was unusual for Kirstin. She handles much more pain than most of us, but this time it was too much. I took the papers and filled them out, but she still had to sign them, because she was over eighteen. This she managed to do, but her signature was as big as the page.

Next she was taken for X-rays, which showed a dislocated elbow. After she was given a local anesthetic, the doctor tried to put her elbow back in place. This proved to be impossible, so he sent us to the hospital in Prescott. There an orthopedic surgeon was called in. Surgery was necessary to fix her elbow.

For weeks, Kirstin was at home with her arm in a cast, collecting workman's comp. When the cast was removed, physical therapy was necessary to restore the use of her arm. This was a little difficult, because Kirstin was afraid her elbow would slip out again. The therapist assured her it wouldn't, but it was hard for her to relax and do the exercises. Still, she made an almost complete recovery.

Kirstin finished the physical therapy, and we waited for the doctor to release her to go back to work. He kept giving us reasons why he wasn't releasing her, but eventually it was obvious he was stalling. He told me that Costco was not required to take Kirstin back. Finally, he did release her. That same afternoon, Kirstin received a call from her manager, asking her to come back to work. She reported for work the very next day. She was obviously valued as a Costco employee.

Shortly after Kirstin returned to work, she was asked to help solve a problem that Costco was having with the food court. The business there had grown to the extent that it was difficult to keep up with the tables, floor, and trash. The employees were busy selling products and were not always able to keep things clean. Kirstin was asked if she would be willing to transfer to that department, and she was offered a raise as well. She was excited about the new opportunity and immediately said yes. We were asked to contact Linda Smith to come in and help Kirstin learn her new job, but before Linda was able to get there, Kirstin had set up her new routine herself. Everything was progressing well for Kirstin in her new position.

This has proved to be an advantageous move for Costco as well as for Kirstin. Her customers (Kirstin calls them members) are constantly thanking her for keeping the food court so clean. One couple told her that they had traveled across the country, stopping at Costco for lunch nearly every day. They had never seen one as clean as hers. She has been recognized many times by a corporate vice president, who awarded her the "Golden Rule Award" for her outstanding customer service. One day I was looking at the bulletin board and noticed there were five comment cards posted there. Three of them were about Kirstin. We can hardly go anywhere without someone coming up to Kirstin and making comments about her work.

Lately, Kirstin's supervisor has been giving her new tasks to learn inside the food court. Each time she is presented with a new challenge, she meets it with enthusiasm and determination. Her supervisor told me that she can show Kirstin one time what to do, and she has it. She excitedly fills us in every day on what she did and what new job she learned. "It's job security. Right, Mom?" She always asks me.

Having a good job is a big part of the American dream. Even as small children, we begin to think about what we will be when we grow up. People with disabilities also have those dreams, but all too often, they are never realized. Kirstin has been fortunate to be able to take advantage of some very good opportunities. She has worked hard to prove that she is worthy of those opportunities. In these trying economic times, Kirstin has been able to stay in her job. Many of her friends have not been so lucky.

Getting a job is a challenge for everyone. For those with disabilities, there are programs in place that should help level the playing field. And they do to some extent. Kirstin was able to utilize Rehabilitative Services for job development and coaching. These services are still available, but finding a job is difficult for everyone these days, and especially for the disabled. I've often wondered why an employer wouldn't take a chance on someone who will be at work every day, on time, follow the rules, and never stop working. Still, they are passed over time and again. I do my best to prepare my students by helping them choose a realistic career goal, design a plan, and develop job-seeking skills. That is the most I can do for them. When they leave, they are at the mercy of prospective employers. They have to be able to sell themselves.

A few of Kirstin's friends have found successful careers. One of her friends, Susan, got a job as a greeter at K-mart. She has a beautiful smile and is naturally friendly, so that took her a long way. But Susan used her own ingenuity to impress her supervisor even more. Customers who had read the sales ad would ask her where they could find certain things that were in the ad. Susan would help them if she could, but this gave her an idea. Every week she took the ad and went around the store. She wrote down the location of the sale items in a notebook. When someone asked for help, she opened her notebook, located the item in the sales ad, and could immediately tell the customer where to find it in the store. Susan's willingness to go the extra mile earned her promotion to receiving clerk.

A parent of one of my former students works at the Veterans Hospital and related a story to me about a man with Down syndrome who works there. Getting the food out was a really busy time, and a man on a restricted diet was almost given the wrong food. It was Kenneth who noticed the mistake and spoke up immediately, preventing a possible catastrophe. Quick thinking might not be a quality usually attributed to people with developmental delays, but attention to detail is. Most of us have so much on our minds that we get distracted. Our special friends have to work harder at focusing on what they are doing. That's why they focus just on the business at hand.

Getting a job is difficult, but keeping it may be even more of a challenge to those with disabilities. This is not because they don't do a good job but because they often become the casualties of a shift in management. The classic case was that of a man named Donald Perkl, who is mentally disabled, autistic, and nonverbal. Through a community vocational rehabilitation program, he was hired by a Chuck E. Cheese restaurant as a maintenance worker. A regional manager was visiting the store and was surprised to find Donald working there. The store manager was told they don't hire "those people." The manager protested, saying that Donald was an excellent employee, and she wanted to keep him. But the regional manager insisted that he be fired.

The US Equal Employment Opportunity Commission (EEOC) sued Chuck E. Cheese on behalf of Donald Perkl due to violations of the Americans with Disabilities Act (ADA) and won. The jury awarded him $13 million in punitive damages and another $70,000 for emotional distress. Unfortunately, the ADA permits a maximum of $300,000, so the award was reduced to that amount. The best news was that Donald was given his job back, and Chuck E. Cheese was ordered to provide training about the requirements of the ADA. General Counsel for the EEOC, Gregory Stewart, said, "This case serves as a clear illustration of the consequences of making employment decisions based on fears and stereotypes, rather that on the qualifications of an individual to perform his job."[1]

---

[1] US Equal Employment Opportunity Commission, "Chuck E. Cheese's Must Pay Maximum Damages Under the ADA to Mentally Retarded Employee following Multi-million Dollar Jury Award" (Washington DC: EEOC, 2000). http://1.eeoc.gov//eeoc/newsroom/release/3-15-00.cfm (accessed July 5, 2011).

Of course this is just one case that ended in court, but the story itself is an all too familiar one. Many of Kirstin's friends have had similar experiences. Local businesses noted for hiring people with disabilities come under new management. One of the first changes made is to eliminate all of "those people." We have witnessed this in supermarkets, sandwich shops, and fast-food restaurants. The workers go quietly back to the sheltered workshops or to look for a new job. For our part, there is nothing we can do except personally boycott the undeserving businesses.

In her time at Costco, Kirstin has worked for four general managers and many direct supervisors. Fortunately, she has not had to prove herself each time there was a change in leadership, but she has had to learn to work under different leadership styles. When it comes to coworkers as well, Kirstin has been able to deal with people who are really friendly toward her and some who aren't. This is the nature of the workplace, and something we all have to learn for ourselves.

Most people with special needs qualify for various types of assistance when it comes to seeking employment. But sometimes the system that is intended to help only makes getting a job more difficult. When Kirstin was receiving Supplemental Social Insurance (SSI), every form they sent us advised us of how to get help if Kirstin wanted to work. The ideal situation is that once a person starts working, SSI could be reduced and eventually eliminated. That is how it worked with Kirstin, but that is not always the case.

A parent of one of my former students told me how her daughter and her daughter's husband quit their jobs. It seems that someone from the Social Security office told the couple that if they quite working, they would receive more in SSI benefits. On that say-so alone, the two quit their jobs. What they were told was correct, but it was not the whole truth. The fact is that when a person works, SSI is reduced by $1 for every $2 earned after the first $85. What the person from Social Security should have said was that you will always make more money if you work than if you just collect SSI alone.

Sometimes circumstances are such that it is in the best interest of the family for the person with a disability not to work. Raising a child who has a disability can be expensive, and families with very limited resources receive assistance from SSI beginning when the child is first diagnosed. Families can become dependent on that income, so allowing the person to get a job becomes more complicated. I have often thought about how expensive it is for the state to maintain someone in a group home. It seems that providing more support for families would make it easier for the person with a disability to remain at home if that is his or her choice. Sometimes one parent has to stay home to provide care or drive the disabled person to work, training, or appointments.

In 2009, the Bureau of Labor Statistics began reporting unemployment rates for people with disabilities. In June of 2011, when the unemployment rate was 9 percent, the unemployment rate for people with disabilities was 16.9 percent. Even more disturbing is the fact that while 70.2 percent of the nondisabled population participated in the workforce, only 21.3 percent of the disabled population participated.[2] It is certain that many of the disabled are not capable of working due to physical or mental limitations, but it is also certain that just as many give up or don't even try because getting a job seems like an impossibility. How many talented, dedicated workers are we throwing away because they are never given the opportunity to show what they can do?

It is Saturday morning; I arrive early to pick Kirstin up for work. This is good, because she has a minor problem. The strap is broken on her purse. "Do you think we have time to stop at Walmart?" she asks.

"If we hurry," I tell her. Once inside Walmart, we locate the handbags. In a matter of minutes, she has selected the one she wants. Back in the car, Kirstin transfers her things to the new purse.

---

[2] US Bureau of Labor Statistics, *Data on the Employment Status of People with a Disability* (Washington DC: Division of Labor Force Statistics, 2010). http://data.bls.gov (accessed July 30, 2011).

"We have twenty minutes, and Costco is five minutes away." I reassure her. As we pull into the Costco parking lot, Kirstin remarks, "I hope it won't be too crazy today."

"It's Saturday," I remind her. "It's bound to be busy." I pull up in front of Costco, and she gets out. "Have a wonderful day," I tell her.

"I'll try," she shoots back over her shoulder as she hurries inside. Such is the life of the working girl.

> ## KIRSTIN'S SIDE OF THE STORY
>
> *I like to do my work every day, and I work hard at it. I like my boss, Kris. She helps me do a good job. I've had my job at Costco for a long time. That's because I'm a good worker. I get a lot of compliments from the members. I care about all the people who come to my food court. I like to be helpful to people with disabilities.*
>
> *It's a lot of fun to work in the food court. Kris calls me "Bubba." She says, "Bubba, go check your area." "Bubba, do the dough balls." "Bubba, we need pizza skins." My coworker Randy calls me "Sweetpea." Kim always tells me, "It's all good in the hood."*
>
> *There are some things I don't like. I don't like it when workers argue. I don't like emptying the trash when it is heavy. But I do like getting paid every two weeks. I look at my pay stub on my computer to see how much money I made. I like getting benefits like health care and my 401K.*
>
> *My advice to someone looking for a job is to be flexible and willing to help people when they need it. Don't be afraid to learn new jobs. It makes you more valuable, and it's job security.*

Chapter Eleven

Driving Me Crazy

Kirstin and I had a thirty-minute commute to Bradshaw Mountain High School every morning and back home to Chino Valley every afternoon. This gave us plenty of time to talk about life and dreams and things that bothered us. One day when we were on our way home, a car came around a curve a little widely, and I had to move over to the dirt edge of the two-lane road I was on. It was a little tense for a few seconds, but when I was safely back on the road, Kirstin told me that she didn't want to drive. She said it would be too scary, because she might have an accident. I told Kirstin I agreed with her decision, and I was proud of her for making such a wise choice that she had obviously spent some time thinking about.

That was one more worry I could check off my list. While other parents were dealing with how to convince their child with special challenges that driving was not a wise choice, I had a very intelligent child who figured it out for herself. There would not be any battles in our house as we tried to explain why driving was a very bad idea. We were lucky to have a daughter with so much common sense.

During Kirstin's senior year, our high school had a program for students with perfect attendance. Every quarter, Kirstin received a free pizza dinner for four or some other perk for having perfect attendance. In the final quarter of the year, there was a big gift giveaway, and all of the students who had perfect attendance drew a prize. There were computers and other electronics, as well as luggage and clothing. There was also a car. It hadn't occurred to me that Kirstin might win the car, but I was very relieved when she opened her envelope to find out she would receive a portable phone.

For the first time at our high school, the graduates were to be treated to a huge overnight party. There were lots of chaperones. Olga, Kirstin's cafeteria boss, and her husband, Steve, who was our football coach and PE teacher, had a son graduating with Kirstin, and they would be there all night. The festivities included music, dancing, and a casino night. The theme was a luau with appropriate food and drinks with umbrellas (no alcohol, of course).

We dropped Kirstin off at the school gym at ten o'clock, when the party started, certain that she would have a great time. At five o'clock the next morning, we received a phone call from Steve, who informed us, "Kirstin won the car at the casino night. What do you want to do with it?"

Suddenly, the idea of driving was not a dead issue. Kirstin owned a car. To make matters worse, one of my students, Angela, was living with us at the time. Angela was seventeen, and one of the things foremost on her mind was getting a license. It became obvious that short of telling Kirstin she could not drive, we were going to have to play this out and see where it went.

We had never told Kirstin she wasn't capable of doing something she really wanted to try, and now she wanted to drive. I immediately came up with a very easy way out of the situation. Kirstin has had vision problems all her life. She wears bifocals to correct strabismus, and without them, she sees double. To get her driver's license, she would have to pass a vision test, and her eyeglasses were like pop bottles. I could take her to the Motor Vehicle Department (MVD), and if things went my way, she would fail the vision test. We would all feel sad for her, and there would be nothing that could be done.

After they had studied the driver's manual for a week, quizzing each other on the information, I took Kirstin and Angela to the MVD in

Prescott. Angela's mother had provided her birth certificate and a signed affidavit so that she could apply for her driving permit. Kirstin, I soon discovered, didn't need any of that. First of all, she was over eighteen and didn't require parental permission. Second, she already had a state identification card and that was all she needed. The next thing I knew, Kirstin was taking her vision test and then they were telling her to go take her test for a permit. I was behind her, stamping my feet, and insisting, "She wasn't supposed to pass the eye test." The MVD worker was laughing her head off. Both girls failed the written test but were told they could return in a week to take it again.

Craig put Kirstin behind the wheel of her car and had her drive around on our property. He said she did fairly well. I couldn't even watch. Angela also practiced driving, and the two girls continued to study the driving manual.

Fortunately, neither Angela nor Kirstin ever passed the written test. But for the next few months, we were taking a trip to the MVD as often as they were allowed to retake the test. Eventually, Angela did get her license when she moved to Minnesota and has been driving for years. For Kirstin, seven tries at the written test were enough for her, and she eventually gave up.

You may be wondering what happened to the little red Nissan Kirstin won. After Michael got married, the newlyweds were only able to afford one car, so Tina, Michael's wife, drove Kirstin's car for a few years. Eventually, Kirstin decided to sell the car for $500. She used the money to buy a new bed. Driving seemed to be a dead issue.

When Kirstin started working at Taco Bell, thoughts of driving came up again. We had to hire drivers for her, and this created some additional problems. Drivers were unreliable and often showed up late. Not to mention that it was expensive. I recall one truly frustrating incident, where Kirstin didn't even make it to work. It was the year of the grasshoppers, and our house was completely surrounded by the giant insects. Kirstin was especially afraid of them and didn't go out of the house until we made sure the path was clear. She was home alone, waiting for her ride, when the driver honked for her to come out. Kirstin went out the back door and was immediately paralyzed at the sight of several huge grasshoppers. Panic set in, and she couldn't move—even when the driver continued to honk. Finally, Kirstin was able to get to the front of the house just in time to see the driver leave. She had to call Taco Bell and tell them she wouldn't be in that day.

Missing work due to grasshoppers seems like a ridiculous excuse, but a more responsible driver might have checked to see why Kirstin didn't come out of the house. This was just one incident, but there were many other times when Kirstin was late for work or didn't get there at all because the driver had a problem.

Taco Bell was only about five miles from our home. We considered that if she had a golf cart, she could drive it down a twenty-five-mile-an-hour road with stop signs every half mile and very little traffic. She would be able to turn into the Taco Bell without ever going out on the highway. The problem we discovered was that in order to drive a golf cart on a public road, she had to meet all the requirements for a driver's license.

A year later, Kirstin was working at Costco. She had to be at work at 5 a.m., so every morning, Craig drove her in. For the first year, she worked every Saturday and Sunday. That meant our weekend had to be arranged around her work schedule. We couldn't go very far away from home, because we only had four hours before we had to be back at Costco to pick her up. I'm sure this is one of the reasons many parents of children with disabilities keep them at home rather than help them get a job. That certainly would have been easier for us, but we were willing to put up with the inconvenience, because working meant so much to Kirstin.

That should have been the end of the story, and for many years it was. Until recently, Kirstin was content to let others drive her places she needed to go. After she and her grandmother became housemates, they purchased a car together. Kirstin qualified equally for the loan, and she shows as an owner on the title. Grandma drove Kirstin to work every day and to all of her afterwork activities, such as her signing group and the chimes choir. On Wednesdays, Kirstin's day off, they went shopping together. It was a very satisfactory arrangement for everyone.

Then a little over a year ago, my mom fell and broke her hip. Thank God it happened after she picked Kirstin up from work and not after she dropped her off. That way, Kirstin was there with her and able to get help right away. Both Craig and Michael showed up and took her to the hospital. There was surgery to repair her hip and a period of convalescence. When she was fully recovered, the doctor cleared her to drive. But fear of falling again brought an end to her days of driving. Craig and I were now their transportation, especially Craig, who wasn't working. This started Kirstin thinking about driving. After all, she does own a car—again. In fact, they made the final payment on the car last year. Now Kirstin owns a 2003 Sunbird, and she wants to drive.

Thoughts of Kirstin driving terrified me, especially thinking of her out on the road alone. What if something happened to the car? What if she got in an accident? No one would be there to help her. For a while, I was unsupportive, thinking that it would blow over. Having been here with other Kirstin ideas, such as going to college and buying a home, I knew I would eventually be overruled. So I was the one who contacted the A-1 Driving School to see what the requirements were and how much it cost. The first step, of course, was to get an instruction permit. The driving school offered a thirty-hour course to prepare her for the test. The cost was $230, and there was a class starting during our school's spring break. Kirstin had just received her tax refund, and she was able to take a week off from work, so all of the details fell into place.

The next thing I knew, I was spending my spring break driving Kirstin to the driving school. After her first class, on Monday, she informed us that she would be taking the written test on Tuesday. This seemed premature to me, and I was sure she would not be able to pass it. As it turned out, I was correct, but she would have two more chances to take the test during the week. Her instructor suggested that I help Kirstin study from the manual and work on the practice questions. She would take the test again on Thursday to give her more time to study.

After she had been in class for six hours, Kirstin and I would spend an additional two hours studying. She was so determined that I was drawn into the project and became fully invested in it. As I drove her to class every morning, I would point out examples of some of the concepts she was having trouble with. There is a roundabout right by Kirstin's home, and lots of people have trouble understanding how it works. It took Kirstin a while, but she did come to see how the driver in the roundabout has the right-of-way. Another fortunate circumstance was the fact that there was a blind intersection near the driving school. Kirstin watched as I inched up and had her peek around the tree that was obstructing our view.

Part of the problem Kirstin had with the rules was caused by the fact that things are so black and white to her. I would ask her, for example, "What is the seat belt rule?" She would say, "You get in the car and put on your seat belt." Over and over, I would say, "That's your rule. What's the one in the driver's manual?" Finally, she was able to recite the rule exactly as it was written in the manual.

Other concepts were a little more difficult. Such as what to do when the light turns green. Of course Kirstin knows that green means go, but what if there are cars or people in the intersection? We made this standing rule that you don't drive over anyone. The part most of us have difficulty with is remembering all the numbers, such as how far to park from a fire hydrant or the distance you must stay behind an emergency vehicle. Kirstin had those down pat in no time.

After class on Thursday, Kirstin remained to take her second shot at the test. Craig and I arrived late to pick her up but still had to wait. Those were tense moments, hoping for the best, whatever we considered that to be. Finally, Kirstin came out, looking dejected and I knew immediately she hadn't passed. "My teacher wants to talk to you," she said and then added, "It's nothing bad."

The state allows the test-taker to miss six answers; Kirstin had missed nineteen. Her teacher had a suggestion that made very good sense to me. She said that there was a Saturday class starting up, and those students would be taking their test on the second Saturday. Kirstin could come on that day and take her test for the third time. That would give her two weeks to prepare. Her teacher warned that if Kirstin did not pass the test, it was unlikely that she would be able to pass it at the MVD. The MVD gives their test on a computer, and it counts down the errors. When the test-taker reaches seven errors, the testing stops. This can be very stressful, and stress seemed to be a factor with Kirstin.

We left the driving school uncertain about what Kirstin wanted to do. At her home, we studied some more, but I was really encouraging her to wait and take her test the following Saturday. Even as I was saying the words, I was sure they were in vain. Kirstin would do what she wanted, and she was really sure she could pass the test on Friday.

Once again, we found ourselves waiting for Kirstin to complete her test, and once again we saw that disappointed look on her face. This time she had only missed nine. One thing I noticed was that Kirstin had missed only one on the first page. Nearly all of her misses were at the end of the test. It seemed that stress really was having an affect on her.

Over the weekend, Kirstin and I studied as much as we could. I told her that in the history of this test, no one was more prepared for it than she was. She could rattle off every answer perfectly. Before work on Monday, her dad took her to the MVD. The instructor recommended that we ask to have the test read to Kirstin. That way she wouldn't be taking it on the computer, and there wouldn't be a countdown. Her first try at the MVD was not successful, although she was pretty close. Kirstin's plan was to return the next day and take the test again.

Unfortunately, on her second try, Kirstin got that MVD worker we have all had at one time or another—the one who acts like you are taking up *her* time. She wasn't going to be bothered with reading the test, so she asked Kirstin a few questions. Her abrupt demeanor frightened Kirstin, who wasn't able answer fast enough to satisfy the worker. Kirstin was sent away to study more and didn't even get a chance to take the test.

As they say, the third time's the charm. And so it was with Kirstin. After her very stressful ordeal, I suggested that she take the test on the computer. This she did, and to her surprise, it suddenly popped up "PASSED." Kirstin was excited, and so were the workers at the MVD. The huge smile on her face on the instruction permit picture says it all.

Once Kirstin had her permit, we were faced with a new challenge: how to get her ready to drive. At first all of her driving took place in parking lots or unused streets. Craig appears to be better able to handle this part than I am. He has more confidence; I have more fears. He took Kirstin to a shopping center that is mostly empty, and Kirstin practiced there for many weeks. There are two levels of streets and lots of empty parking spaces. I took her to a neighborhood where streets were put in but no houses so far. Kirstin did very well, and I tried to relax. It was hard to resist grabbing the wheel, even though we were in no danger. She was only going about fifteen miles per hour. I made her use the turn signal, even though there were no other cars. After our practice, Kirstin touched my arm and said, "You did a lot better today, Mom."

Little by little, Craig eased her out into the streets. She has driven from their practice parking lot to her workplace at Costco. Kirstin has even driven up to the gas pumps and pumped her own gas. She can pull into parking places without hitting any cars. Backing out is another matter. More practice is required. It is still hard for me to imagine Kirstin driving, and my old fears still remain, but I am resigned to the fact that it is inevitable. My oldest grandson now has his instruction permit, and driving is coming much more easily to him. He will probably have his driver's license within a month or two. Kirstin has been working at it for a year. The one thing we can always count on with Kirstin is that she never gives up.

Kirstin does have a few friends who drive. They do very well and don't have many mishaps. One of her friends was stopped by a policeman and given a sobriety test. He had not been drinking, but his jerky movements and rapid speech made the officer think that he had. When he told me about it, I was outraged, but he just seemed to take it in stride.

Transportation is a major problem for Kirstin and all of her friends. It is their biggest consideration when they need to be somewhere. They may be able to get a ride, but that is often complicated. With gas prices as they are, fewer people are willing to go out of their way to pick someone up or take someone home. Being willing to chip in for gas makes it a little easier, but time is a factor for most of us as well.

In our community, public transportation is very limited and not always consistent. This is not only a concern for our special needs friends, but also for the many senior citizens who reside in our area. To count on public transportation to get to work is not realistic. The only option is taking a taxi. Even at Kirstin's pay rate of $20 an hour, she would have to work the first hour and fifteen minutes of every day to pay for a taxi trip to work and back. For those making minimum wage, this would be out of the question. Sometimes there are transportation vouchers available to those who qualify, but they are limited and mostly intended to provide transportation to doctor's appointments, not to work on a daily basis.

Even group homes are feeling the pinch. As gas prices rise, they are finding it necessary to limit the number of places they can take their residents. That means choosing the activities they will participate in with care. It also restricts the choices, because taking only one person to an event is not cost-effective. That means majority rules when it comes to outside activities that require transportation.

Some of Kirstin's friends resort to walking or riding bikes. This is an excellent way to get around during the day and if they don't have to go too far. Nighttime poses new problems. Walking or riding a bike at night is, of course, more dangerous due to less visibility. In addition, many of our friends with special needs live in apartments in older sections of town, where walking at night could be risky.

Public transportation has been recognized as a problem in our communities for a long time. I have personally served on committees that were supposed to work on this problem, but they usually ended with nothing getting done except a decision to have a study done to determine our needs. Now that our population has reached a level to qualify for state and federal assistance, it is our hope that more will be done. Of course, the economy makes that unlikely in the near future.

In the meantime, private transportation companies are trying to fill the needs as much as possible.

As for Kirstin, this is a part of her story that will remain unfinished for a while. Is a driver's license in her future? I believe it is. Will I continue to worry every time she drives? Of course; it goes with the territory.

Recently, Kirstin and I had a girls' day out. Part of our plan was to have her practice driving. On the way to our practice location, I told Kirstin I was still having a hard time picturing her driving by herself. As she put the car into gear and pulled out on the road, I felt the same urge to grab the wheel. Although she got off to sort of a rough start, she soon settled in and drove just fine. At the end of the practice, she asked if I could picture her driving by herself. I said that I couldn't quite see it but to keep practicing, and my vision would probably improve.

KIRSTIN'S SIDE OF THE STORY

Accidents do happen, and I didn't want to drive at first, because it was too scary for me. I don't want to make myself sick by worrying about my driving anyway. I remember when I went to my graduation party. I was shocked that I won a car. I had fun at the overnight party. I enjoyed the music, dancing, and casino night.

I do have a problem with my vision, but that doesn't stop me from driving. I have a driving permit, and my dad and I practice as much as we can. I do own a car. I want to drive so much. I feel bad that my grandma can't drive anymore. I am lucky that my dad takes me to work. My mom doesn't have to be afraid for me. But she came around and helped me go to the A-1 Driving School. I enjoyed the class. I had to study every day with my mom for my written test. My mom showed me a lot of signs on the streets. I know the rules of the streets.

They gave me a week to prepare for my written test. I did the best I could. The computer wasn't easy for me at first, and the MVD worker wasn't helpful to me. I finally passed my written test. I got my permit. My mom fears for me, even though she got my dad to help me practice my driving every day. I learn from the best with my parents. I do understand how difficult it is to drive.

My friends and I always do our best to get to places. The taxis are expensive anyway. The gas prices don't make it any easier on us. When I get my license, I can be more independent. I can go shopping or to David's house when I want to. I won't need someone to drive me to work. Then my dad can have some time off.

Chapter Twelve
ಬಿಲಿ
How Can Our Nest Be Empty?

*E*very challenge has its rewards, and every opportunity has its tradeoffs. One of the tradeoffs I had counted on was that Kirstin would always be with us. Michael was an independent young man at an early age, playing with his friends all day. When we moved to Prescott Valley, he became an adventurer, exploring the creeks and hills around our town. In high school, now a licensed driver, he spent time with his buddies or worked at various part-time jobs. He no longer accompanied us on family vacations. After high school, Michael took a job with the US Forest Service as a firefighter. At first he remained in Chino Valley, but he was soon transferred to other ranger stations in remote areas of our large state. Eventually, he got married and became a parent himself. He had gradually become less and less a part of our daily lives, but Kirstin was always there. She was with us every day and everywhere we went. Other parents had to prepare for having their children move away, but not us. While we knew Kirstin would have a life of her own in some ways, I always assumed she would continue to live with us.

That was why I didn't take her seriously when Kirstin started talking about getting her own place. She had been working at Costco for five years and was pretty well established there. She was working from 11 a.m. until 3 p.m., five days a week. Every morning Craig or I would drop her off at her grandmother's house in Prescott on our way to work. Then a cab would take her to her job. I picked her up from work on my way home from school. This meant that she only needed the taxi one way, which was about $10 for the fifteen-minute drive.

My mom was planning to retire and then she would drive Kirstin to work, thus saving the cost of the cab. It was during those daily commutes that they began to cook up a plan to buy a mobile home together. When they started talking to Craig and me about their idea, I went along with it, all the time thinking that it would never happen. We started visiting mobile home sales lots and looking at the models. Sometimes we talked with the salesperson there, but that is as far as we went. And that was as far as I expected it would ever go. In my mind, there was no way Kirstin would be able to qualify for a mortgage. Since my mom couldn't do it on her own, we would give it a try, and eventually the idea would be forgotten—just like Kirstin's idea of driving a car.

Their plan was perfectly logical. We wouldn't have to drive Kirstin into Prescott every day, which would simplify our lives considerably. Kirstin and Grandma would be good company for each other, and it would give Kirstin an opportunity to be semi-independent. We had talked about Kirstin moving in with a roommate; why couldn't her roommate be her grandmother? Still, I wasn't ready to give up my little girl. I didn't tell Craig how I felt, because I knew they already had his full support.

We continued to look at mobile homes, but there was another issue. Where would they put it if they were able to buy one? There were not very many lots zoned for mobile homes in our area, and the neighborhoods where mobile homes were allowed were not very nice communities. We drove through neighborhoods filled with old, rundown, single-wide mobile homes and thought about safety issues. Neighborhoods with beautiful, double-wide mobiles had all kinds of expensive requirements that were beyond their price range.

The idea was to find a mobile home with a split floor plan. That way Kirstin could occupy one side, and her grandmother would be on the other side, with common areas in the middle. On one of the visits to a mobile home lot, we did find a mobile that would fit their needs and was in their price range. They even filled out paperwork to apply for a loan. The problem was Kirstin only had a credit card, and she needed two forms of credit to qualify. Well, that was a nice try. Too bad it didn't work out.

That seemed like the end of the line as far as getting a loan, until someone thought of the credit union. My mom had her account there for many years, and Kirstin also had a savings account with them. The credit union looked at Kirstin's income and credit history and decided she deserved a chance. The next thing I knew, they had a loan.

Just as quickly, the problem of where to put the home was solved. My mother was renting a mobile home at the time, and the park where she lived also rented lots to people who owned their mobiles. Coincidentally, an old rental had been moved off a lot, and it was now available. With another stroke of a pen, Kirstin and her grandmother were now renters of that property. No other obstacles lay in their path, and before I knew it, their brand-new mobile was delivered and set up. Now there was nothing left to do but move them in.

The empty nest idea didn't fully hit me for a few months. It was May, and it was Mother's Day. On any other Mother's Day, Kirstin would have been parked outside our bedroom door, waiting for us to wake up and open the door so she could rush in present and card in hand. But on this particular Mother's Day, there was no shuffling noise coming from under our door. It hit me like a ton of bricks. We were empty nesters. That was when the tears came.

Kirstin and her grandmother set out to make up their own routines. The floor plan is what they were hoping for: a split. Mom occupies the master bedroom on one side of the house, and Kirstin has the two bedrooms, both with walk-in closets, and the additional bathroom on the other side of the house. In the middle are the living room, dining area, and kitchen. Kirstin chose one room to be her bedroom, and the other room she calls her sitting room. There she has a futon, her TV, karaoke machine, and computer. It is in that room that she does her singing and dancing every morning. It's an important part of her routine.

How to handle the finances was another issue. Together, Kirstin and her grandmother created a budget. They decided that each of them needed to put in $800 a month to cover the house payment, lot rent, insurance, utilities, and car expenses. They would buy groceries together and take turns paying each week. Certain personal food items and health and beauty aids would be paid for individually. They would also take turns filling the gas tank. This all seemed very equitable to us, and so began Kirstin's new life away from home.

Some months later, I came to fully understand how independent Kirstin had become. I was talking to her on the phone, and she said she had a couple of problems she needed help with. First of all, she had gone to the optometrist in Costco to get new glasses. After work, she had made an appointment and gone by herself, filling out all the paperwork. She selected and ordered her new glasses, but she was concerned about the prescription. Kirstin knew that she needed prisms in her glasses to correct the strabismus, but it did not say "prisms" on her prescription. I told her I was sure that the optometrist knew what he was doing. If there was an error and her glasses weren't correct, they would make her new ones.

The other problem she had was that she waited too long to mail her credit card payment, and she wanted me to ask her dad to pay it online from her account, which he had done for her before. I told her I would be happy to do that.

It struck me that this conversation was so ordinary. We could have been any mother and adult daughter talking on the phone. Kirstin's problems could have been those of any young woman out on her own for the first time. Had I ever expected to have such a conversation with Kirstin? The next day I related the whole incident to one of my friends. She agreed that, indeed, the conversation was very typical. "I've had many conversations like that with my daughter," she told me. "The only difference is usually my daughter is asking for money to pay her credit card bill."

As with any two people who live together, Kirstin and her grandmother have their share of disagreements and misunderstandings. Kirstin sometimes uses us as a sounding board, but usually doesn't want us to intercede. "I can handle it myself," she tells us. As her grandmother has had some health problems in the last few years, Kirstin has taken on more responsibilities. She does this most of the time without complaint. One time when my brother and his family were visiting from Colorado, my brother had gotten several pizzas for the crowd for dinner. Everyone ate their fill and moved to the living room. I noticed Kirstin, cleaning up and putting away the leftovers. We had been talking for about forty-five minutes when someone mentioned that we needed to put away the food. "No we don't," I said. "Kirstin took care of it long ago."

What Kirstin gives to us is something priceless. It is peace of mind. We know that Mom, who is now eighty-five, is never alone for more than a few hours a day. If she falls or has a heart problem, Kirstin is there and can call for help as she has done on a few occasions. It allows my mother to remain at home and independent instead of living in a care facility or shuffled around among her children. My brother, sister, and I owe Kirstin a huge debt we will never be able to repay. Our other children have gone about their own lives and visit Grandma when they can. Kirstin has taken on the day-to-day needs and has put her own plans on hold.

This is her home, and she takes responsibility for what needs to be done. She does have her share of mishaps, like the time she set something hot on the counter and burned a spot on it. The fact is, though, we have all done things that cause damage or breakage. It goes with being human. I always wonder at parents who take one mistake by their child who has special needs as an indication that he or she is not capable of doing things like cooking. I've been cooking since I was twelve, and I still burn things once in a while. Kirstin has as much right to make mistakes as anyone.

In the earlier years with Kirstin and her grandmother, they enjoyed their weekly shopping trips on Wednesdays, Kirstin's day off. Since my mother's health problems have made it more difficult for her to get around, most of the actual shopping has fallen on Kirstin. They make a list together and then Craig drives Kirstin to the store. She is a great shopper, who finds good bargains and healthier versions of things. I enjoy going with her when I'm not working. I really learn a lot. It won't be long, I'm afraid, before Kirstin will be driving herself on these weekly trips. But we can always have a girls' day out.

While Kirstin was still living at home, she had spent a few weekends alone while Craig and I went on some mini vacations. This had been a good test of Kirstin's ability to take care of herself. She never had any problems, and we became increasingly more confident in her abilities. The real test of her independence came a few years after she had been living with her grandmother. My mom needed bypass surgery and was in the hospital for several weeks. At first, Kirstin came to stay with us, but after a few weeks, she wanted to be at home. During that time, Kirstin prepared her own meals and took care of all of her needs. Either Craig or I picked her up for work and returned her to her home after work. Other than taking her shopping, she didn't really need any help. I am confident that Kirstin is capable of living on her own should the opportunity ever arise.

Of course Kirstin has no intention of living on her own. Her goal is to marry her fiancé, David. They talk about it constantly and plan their wedding. Kirstin also insists on telling everyone that she is engaged. Which she is, in fact. David proposed to her at an OASIS meeting, down on one knee in front of their friends. Kirstin has framed pictures to prove it.

Unfortunately, there are complications. One problem Kirstin has is that she is a signer on a mortgage. She owns the mobile jointly with her grandmother, so she cannot decide for herself who will live there. Besides the financial obligation, Kirstin has accepted a responsibility to be her grandmother's roommate. She can't just sell the property, split the profits, and go her own way. Someday that might happen, but for now, it is not an option. These are not typical problems faced by someone who wants to get married, but there are probably other thirty-six-year-olds who have similar situations. As always, Kirstin is patient and willing to wait for what she wants.

Once in a while, Kirstin comes to stay with us for a few days. This is usually because my brother or sister is visiting, and the mobile is crowded with family members. On those occasions, I invite Kirstin to be a guest with us. We set up the AeroBed in our spare room (Kirstin's old bedroom), just like we do for any other houseguest. Kirstin likes to pitch in with the cooking, and I enjoy spending time with her in the kitchen. After dinner, she always wants to play a card game we enjoy called Pounce. It is played with two decks of cards. The game is played like solitaire, except we each have seven cards that are the "pounce pile." We play on each other's aces and try to put up as many cards as possible, while also getting rid of the cards in the pounce pile one by one. The first person to do that yells, "Pounce," with the hope of catching the opponent with all seven cards. The game requires paying attention to a lot of different areas at once and is stressful, because everything changes so quickly. We play until someone has a hundred points, and that someone is always me—that is until the last time we played. Kirstin's skills have continued to improve, and I have to admit she beat me. Playing Pounce with her will never be the same again.

Because Kirstin has been at Costco for thirteen years, she receives quite a bit of vacation time. Craig and I try to make sure that we take her on a vacation once a year, as going on a trip by herself is not possible. When Grandma was able to travel, it was the four of us. The last few years, it has been just us three. I offer some suggestions about where to go, and we all discuss the possibilities. Then we come to a consensus. Kirstin helps pay for some of the expenses along the way. One her favorite ways to contribute is to take her parents out to a fancy restaurant for dinner. Sometimes we go to Disneyland or somewhere else in California. Other times we have gone on longer road trips through several states and even on a cruise. Kirstin is a great traveler and lots of fun. She is always excited about everything.

Living with a roommate was something Kirstin considered before she and her grandmother became housemates. I'm not sure how that would have worked out, but some of her friends have tried it with undesirable results. For the men, it tends to turn out better, but for her women friends, not so well. There seem to be more conflicts with women and disagreements over who is going to do what. I have a little program I use with my students to help prepare them for being roommates just in case that might happen in the future. It covers things like who should get the biggest bedroom, how to split up the space in the refrigerator, and what things are personal and what can be shared. There are so many things we do for our children on a daily basis that we don't even realize. We make many decisions that they will be making on their own when they move out. The more we can prepare them, the better chance they have for a smooth transition. I've seen situations where some of Kirstin's friends went out to dinner together, and someone who was newly on her own didn't realize she needed to bring money to pay for her own meal. She had never had to do that.

Preparation for independent living can never start too soon. Kirstin had an allowance at an early age. She has been making financial decisions ever since. Once she was eligible for SSI, Kirstin had a checking account of her own into which the payments were deposited. With help from us, she managed those funds from the start. Kirstin began picking up the tab occasionally when we dined out. She knows that you put your debit card in the folder, and when the server comes back with the bill, you have to add on the tip. Going out to dinner with some of her friends from Costco has never been a problem for her, because she knows just what to do.

Roommates often don't know each other that well before moving in together. Finding out that your roommate is comfortable living in a messy apartment when you are a neat freak is going to lead to some serious confrontations. What if you're an early riser, like Kirstin, and your roomy is a night owl? Someone might like quiet, and the roommate is very noisy and talkative. These things might work out but not on their own. I think a lot of groundwork needs to be done if roommates are to live together successfully.

Watching your child venture out into the world without you for the first time is difficult for any parent, but for the parent of a child with special needs, it borders on nightmarish. I am sure that is why many parents choose to keep their child at home with them forever. Each situation is unique, and we try to make the best decisions for our children. But we also have to be brave and trust them to help us find what is best. After the physical and emotional investments we have made in our children, putting them in a group home sometimes seems like failing them in the end. But that is in no way true. Group homes are a wonderful opportunity for a person with developmental challenges to live her own life. I have had friends whose children have chosen to live in group homes. Their lives are filled with friendships and activities they enjoy. In our area, there are a few ranches devoted to adults with special needs. I have met some of the residents, and they seem happy and fulfilled. When they go home to visit their families, the time together is special and they have stories to tell.

Parents who have a special needs child later in life may be in the situation where the child will probably outlive the parents by many years. These families often make plans and arrangements for the inevitable. Sometimes, though, decisions must be made by other family members after the death of a parent. The family may feel a sense of obligation to provide for the person with special needs, so that person is shuffled from family member to family member. There are many alternatives out there, and they should all be considered. Supporting your child in his or her decision about where to live as an adult helps both parents and child move on to the next phase of their lives.

Adults with special needs who remain at home often find themselves involved in every activity that comes along. The parent becomes the extension of the soccer mom, who spends her days driving her child from one event to the next every week. Obviously, the parent has good intentions, but sometimes this may not be what the person with special needs wants to be doing. As parents, we are so used to making the decisions that we forget to ask, or maybe we just don't listen. When Kirstin chose to give up the signing group she was in, I fought her over it. I did ask her why she wanted to quit, and she gave me a perfectly acceptable answer. Raising her arms and making the gestures bothered her joints. She has had problems with her joints and even dislocated her elbow at work, so what she was saying made sense. But I continued to question her, convinced that she was quitting under pressure from David, who was no longer in the signing class. Time and again, Kirstin reassured me that her decision had nothing to do with David, but I was having trouble accepting what I was being told. In my mind, Kirstin was giving up something she really enjoyed, and she would come to regret it. I now realize that Kirstin knew exactly what she was giving up and that she was comfortable with her decision. Seeing how much she enjoys watching the signing group perform, I know that she has no regrets.

As parents, Craig and I are as proud of Kirstin and her accomplishments as we are of our son Michael. They have both made their own way in the world as strong, successful, independent adults. Kirstin knows her own mind and will stand up for what she thinks is best for her (even to her overbearing mother). Letting go is a very difficult thing to do, and I don't think we have fully mastered it yet. Maybe we never will. But Kirstin is always patient with us and helps us learn to be better empty nesters.

KIRSTIN'S SIDE OF THE STORY

I like being independent. Growing up means having a lot of responsibilities. I have a mortgage to pay with my grandmother. I like having my own home and my own car. There is a lot of paperwork to do when you buy a house. We got a loan from the credit union. I am happy that I have a good credit history.

I budget my money carefully. I have lots of bills to pay. It is not always easy being an adult. My mom says we all make mistakes, and that is okay as long as we learn from them. I am a good cook. I keep my house clean. I am a good shopper.

I do worry about my grandmother. I help her as much as I can. We have disagreements at times. My grandmother and I have to be patient with each other. We always love each other, even when we disagree. We have each other no matter what.

All children have their families, even when they grow up. My mom and I play Pounce together, cook together, and spend time together. We don't see each other every day, but that makes it more special when we are together.

We all make our choices in life, even though they might not be the right ones. I love David, but we have our share of problems. David and I will still get married, even though we have our own obligations. We have faith that it will happen someday.

Chapter Thirteen

ఞ ఁ

Modern Problems

One day when Kirstin was working in the bakery at Costco, I arrived to pick her up, expecting her to be sitting on the bench outside as usual. When I didn't see her there, I went inside the store and sat at a table in the food court. After a half hour had gone by and still no Kirstin, I walked back to the bakery to try to find her. Kirstin was there, working furiously on something. She said, "This is the worst day of my life. I have to get these done. I'm probably going to get fired."

With that she went back into the bakery, and I was left to continue waiting. While I waited, I started thinking about how Kirstin had to deal with adult problems and how her life was difficult. Was it fair to put her in such a situation? She could be at home, collecting Social Security and having an easy life. Then I realized I didn't choose this; Kirstin did. She wasn't choosing to take the easy way out; it wasn't in her blood to do that. She came from a long line of hard workers on both sides of her family. Craig and I both lost our fathers when we were babies, and our mothers had to enter the workforce in order to provide for us. Kirstin inherited their work ethic, and over the years, we have instilled it in her as we have in her brother. She was just doing what came naturally to her and what she had learned from example. Kirstin accepted responsibility for completing her work. She did finish—about an hour late. She didn't lose her job, and the incident was never repeated.

As a teacher, I have seen plenty of times when parents bail their children out of situations. Right or wrong, I think we have to look carefully at what we are doing and what kind of message we are sending. In life, we are held accountable for our actions.

Of course there are safety issues with all children and especially with our special children. That leads us to the question of how much we can protect them and how much we should protect them. There are no easy answers, but the choices we make as parents can enable our children or disable them. The fact is that no matter how much we want to, we can never protect our children from everything. We can't protect them from the loss of a loved one, from accidents or illness, or from natural disasters. In trying to protect them from every rude person they might encounter or from stressful situations we aren't really helping them. It is the day-to-day frustrations that we all deal with that make us strong. Those are the things that prepare us for the bigger problems that we must face from time to time.

We have tried to keep Kirstin safe but also allow her to explore the world. We have chosen to encourage her to live her life rather than always play it safe. In school, Kirstin rode the regular school bus. Sometimes there were problems with teasing, and she had to stand up for herself. One experience was especially challenging. There was a boy on Kirstin's bus who tried to get her to go home with him. His intentions were not good, and we were frightened for Kirstin, because she had a half-mile walk from the bus stop to our home. But we were also relieved that Kirstin knew she needed to tell us what happened. We contacted the police, and they sent an officer to the boy's home. Kirstin continued to ride the bus, and the boy eventually left her alone.

Years later, when a man at Costco was touching Kirstin a little more than she was comfortable with, she was able to handle it herself by talking to her supervisor. The experience in middle school helped her understand what to do and gave her the confidence in herself to do it.

The year Kirstin went to Yavapai College, there was a rapist on the campus. Female students who lived in the dorm were being escorted home after evening classes by members of the basketball team. Of course we were concerned about Kirstin's vulnerability. But instead of pulling her out of college, we armed her with knowledge about what to do. All the way to the school I recited a litany of rules: "Don't talk to men you don't know. Don't go into the parking lot with anyone. Stay where there are lots of people." Kirstin was a little disgusted that I felt the need to repeat these rules every day and assured me that she knew what to do.

More than once, I sat in my car and watched her walk across the Costco parking lot at 5 a.m., ring the bell on the door, and get swallowed up by the huge warehouse. There was a moment when I wanted to call her back to the safety of my arms. But I never did. This was her world now, and while I was still a part of her world, I would never again be her whole world.

After high school, Kirstin joined a self-advocacy group called OASIS—Organized Adults with Special Needs in Society. OASIS was created by the ARC of Arizona, an organization dedicated to the advancement of people with developmental disabilities. The sponsor for the Prescott OASIS was Kirstin's friend, Jean McGuire. Prescott OASIS met in a church meeting room once a month for a business meeting followed by a guest speaker. Their speakers were usually adults with special challenges who talked about how they were able to overcome those challenges. Their favorite guest speaker was Tom Whittaker, who was the first person with a disability to climb Mount Everest. Tom lost his right foot in an auto accident in 1979. He wears a prosthetic foot and even took it off for the OASIS members and passed it around so they could examine it more closely. It took him three tries in three years to reach the summit of Mount Everest. With him on his attempts were many other people with physical disabilities who were only able to make it to base camp. Tom was an inspiration to the OASIS members, who also have dreams and much to overcome in reaching those dreams.

The ARC of Arizona was busy setting up OASIS groups around the state, and Kirstin was sometimes invited to help start a new chapter. This was an opportunity for her to travel and meet new people. Once each year a convention was held somewhere in the state, and Kirstin's group attended. Most of the conventions were held at hotels. If they came to Prescott, we went to a camp. The sessions were based on the interests of the OASIS members and included workshops on employment, marriage, finances, and how to obtain services. There were also fun workshops with crafts, singing, and exercise. On Saturday evening, there would be a banquet with a guest speaker and awards.

One year, the guest speaker was a young woman with Down syndrome from New Mexico. She was a dynamic speaker named Nannie Marie Sanchez, who was very moving as she talked about her dreams and encouraged the others to never give up. The conference was being held at a camp in Prescott, which meant that it was a little more casual. Kirstin was able to spend some time with Nannie, and they immediately started talking like old friends. It was the first time I had seen Kirstin with such a kindred spirit, and it was amazing to watch them. The young woman from New Mexico wanted to drive and had completed a certificate program at her local community college. Kirstin had also spent a year in college, so they compared horror stories. Kirstin wasn't thinking about driving at the time, but she had been working at Costco for a few years and felt successful. I wished they lived closer so they could see each other more often, but that was their only meeting.

One of the workshops at the convention was on political awareness. There were quite a few adults with special needs attending the session, where they learned about the political system and voting. At the end of the session, anyone who wanted to register to vote was asked to go to a table to complete the paperwork. Craig and I were enlisted to help, as there was quite a line of people wanting to register. I was helping a woman who was very excited about becoming a registered voter. When I got to the question about being declared incompetent, I found out that her parents had been appointed her legal guardians. In that case, she was not eligible to vote. This proved to be the case with over half of those waiting to register. It was difficult to tell them that they didn't have the right to vote as other adults do.

Kirstin has been a registered voter since she was eighteen, and she has voted in every election. We usually talk about how we are going to vote and come to some consensus in our family, but there have been times when Kirstin and I canceled each other out by voting opposite ways. She always has a mind of her own. Guardianship was not something we ever considered for Kirstin. If she had chosen to go into a group home, we would most certainly have become her guardians, as she might have been too easily manipulated by her caregivers if she didn't have someone to protect her. As it is, Kirstin handles her own finances. She is able to make decisions for herself about driving, getting married, and so on. She asks us for advice, but the choice is ultimately hers. I feel fortunate that this has worked out well so far.

On a hot, June day, shortly after Kirstin's eighteenth birthday, we had a girls' day out that wasn't what Kirstin would call fun. Our first stop was the Social Security office, where she applied for SSI. She was not eligible for those benefits before, because our family income was too high. But now that she was eighteen, only her income was considered. We learned that her benefits would be about $560 a month. Next we went to the bank, so she could open a checking account. To meet the requirements of the Social Security program, the account had to be in my name for Kirstin. That was how we set it up, but only her name would appear on the checks, and only she would have a debit card.

Our final stop was the MVD. There we were able to accomplish two tasks. First of all, Kirstin became a brand-new registered voter. Then we waited for her number to be called, so she could apply for a state identification card. The picture on her original ID card tells the whole tale. It looks like someone who is totally disgusted with being dragged around town all day.

From the start, Kirstin handled her own checking account and expenses. Later, when she started working, we charged her for gas and some living expenses so that she would be able to keep more of her SSI payments, but otherwise, she made the decisions about how to spend her money. This she did with amazingly good sense. She had learned how to keep a check register and write checks in the independent living class in high school. She quickly put that knowledge to work for real.

The first office Kirstin held in the OASIS club was treasurer. She was responsible for keeping track of a few thousand dollars, and she took that responsibility very seriously. I set her account up on a Quicken program, and she became very good at keeping records and preparing monthly reports. One day I was walking by as she was on the computer. I heard her say, "Now all I have to do is reconcile. Then I can print my report." I could tell she had learned very well.

Many times I have envied Kirstin's natural common sense when it comes to money matters. One such time was the day she received a prequalification offer from American Express. "Look," I showed her, "you could get an American Express card. Imagine that." Of course my motive was to have some future bragging rights, as I told my friends that Kirstin had an American Express card. Kirstin, on the other hand, was more cautious. "I'll think about it," she said. The next time I came over to her house, she handed the application back, telling me, "I don't really need this." *Why can't I be that wise?* I wondered. I could have saved myself many years of trying to pay off credit cards "I really didn't need."

At another OASIS conference in Prescott, I sat with the mother of Kirstin's boyfriend as they attended a workshop on marriage. We looked at each other and said, "Do you think they can get married?" We never had to answer that question, because a year later, they broke up. But Kirstin would soon have another boyfriend, and the thought of marriage would reappear even more seriously. One year the guest speakers were a married couple who had a successful relationship as well as employment success. They were role models for the others who wanted the same.

Many of my former students have gotten married, and some of the marriages have been successful. Marriage is difficult for everyone, and it is especially difficult when there are disabilities to overcome as well as the usual challenges of day-to-day life. In some cases, both spouses had disabilities. In some ways, that works out better, because they need and usually get support. When one spouse has disabilities and one does not, the nondisabled spouse usually bears all of the responsibilities. This may work for a while, but the burden is sometimes too much, and the marriage ends.

One of my former students surprised everyone when she announced that she was married. She and her boyfriend were working at YEI. One day they returned from lunch as a married couple. The Yavapai County Courthouse is within walking distance (not an easy walk) of YEI. Apparently they had gone there to get a marriage license and scheduled their wedding. Then they returned a few days later to be married. The couple moved into the Head Hotel in downtown Prescott, and there they lived together as man and wife, going to work each day at YEI.

While being married is a struggle, having children creates even greater problems. Fortunately for us, Kirstin decided long ago that having children would not be something she is capable of. When someone is visiting who has a baby, Kirstin is content to make comments about how cute the baby is. She doesn't usually ask to hold the baby though. It seems a blessing that Kirstin feels no loss at not having children. She is content to be an aunt to our three grandchildren. I always feel sorry for those young women who want children so badly but will never be capable of caring for them.

Some of my former students do have children, and in some cases, it has worked out fine. Their families accept the situation and help them handle the responsibilities of parenthood. At other times, there is a struggle within the family, and the result is a break between parents and the mother who has special needs. Then there is no support system in place to help the young mother. Sometimes this results in the state taking the children away.

Kirstin receives many benefits from working at Costco. Among them are health, vision, and dental insurance. Company health insurance has become more important in the last several years, because she no longer qualifies for Medicaid. I can't even imagine what it would cost to purchase health insurance for her. After working for Costco for ten years, Kirstin qualified for long-term care insurance as well.

Another important benefit she receives is life insurance. When Kirstin was a young child, we tried to purchase a life insurance policy like the one we had for her brother. It was a small policy that could be converted to a larger policy when he became an adult, and it guaranteed insurability. We were told that Kirstin was not eligible for such a policy, because she has Down syndrome. We didn't know that in the 1970s, the median life expectancy for someone with Down syndrome was twelve months.

Over the years, the life expectancy of someone with Down syndrome has increased drastically. It is now close to age fifty, and after the child reaches his first birthday, the life expectancy goes up to age sixty. Even with the changing statistics, it is difficult if not impossible to buy life insurance for someone with Down syndrome.

I'm sure that the change in life expectancy is due largely to the fact that babies born with Down syndrome are being raised at home with their families. They are stimulated and encouraged by people who care about them deeply. Postnatal care today is so much better than it was in the 1970s. Doctors have many more lifesaving procedures at their disposal. I think there is also a different attitude toward the value of a human life, even when there are challenges. Parents and doctors are willing to go to extraordinary lengths to make sure babies survive.

One insensitive man I was talking to on the phone asked me if Kirstin looked like someone who was middle-aged. Kirstin was in her early twenties at the time, and I assured him that she looked quite young for her age. What I wish I had said to him was that Kirstin was still occasionally being offered crayons and coloring pages by the hostess when we ate in a restaurant. This was especially likely when our grandchildren were with us. I suggested to Kirstin that when someone did that she should say, "No, I don't need any crayons, but I would like a beer." I thought the shock value as the server checked her identification would be priceless. But Kirstin would never do it.

After Kirstin had been working at Costco for a few years, she was invited to join their 401K program. I helped her fill out the necessary forms. Costco would match up to 8 percent of her salary, so it made sense to make her contributions 8 percent. The major decision to be made was what type of investment she wanted. I was thinking she should put some of her money in a secure annuity and the rest in mutual funds or stocks. Kirstin said no to that. She wanted her entire portfolio in Costco stock. This seemed like a risky idea to me, but she was certain that was what she wanted.

Over the years, Kirstin's decision has paid off so much that I wish I let her do my investing. I was looking at her most recent statement and saw she gained $5,000 in one quarter. It was a gain of nearly 10 percent. Although we have plenty of life insurance that will help take care of Kirstin if we pass away first, I always felt that we should have set aside money for Kirstin to live on when she is older. Now I see that Kirstin is doing that herself. She will be able to retire and continue to be independent. Her resources will make her ineligible for SSI, but she will be able to collect Social Security when she retires, like almost everyone else.

When Jean McGuire moved to California, Craig became the sponsor of the Prescott OASIS. This was a good position for him. He is patient and doesn't try to control things. I didn't attend the monthly meetings and tried to stay away as much as possible, because the teacher in me would always come out, and I would end up being too bossy. Craig had more of a laissez-faire approach, letting the elected officers run the meetings while he sat back and watched. For the most part, the meetings went smoothly, and they were able to complete their business quickly. The vice president was responsible for lining up a speaker for after the business meeting.

Leaving things in the hands of the officers and members did lead to confusion at times. If Craig had been more on top of things, he probably would have found out sooner that he had passed away. We were never able to track down how the rumor started, but since many of the officers worked at YEI, my guess is that it started there. After that, it spread by telephone until finally it reached Craig's cosponsor, Tom. That was how we found out. It was interesting that no one felt it necessary to check out the story. They all believed it and passed it on. Craig said just like Mark Twain, "The rumors of my death have been greatly exaggerated."

Jean had left them with some traditions that Craig made sure they carried on. One of those traditions was the recognition of birthdays. Each member who had a birthday that month came forward with a penny for each year of his age. As the other members counted out loud, the one with the birthday deposited the pennies. This they did proudly and with enthusiasm, even when they were counting to numbers in the forties and fifties. I have witnessed that many times and wondered how comfortable I would be having my age broadcast in such a public way. I'm pretty sure it isn't something they do at the Rotary Club.

Another tradition they continued was the summer soirée. This was usually held at a local park and included a huge sub sandwich. Because it also represented the birthday of Prescott OASIS, there was a big birthday cake as well. It became Kirstin's job to order the cake at Costco. Usually Craig would order the sub sandwich, but one year the president volunteered to take care of that duty. We were all waiting at Goldwater Lake, but he didn't arrive with the food. He finally showed up over an hour late with a story to tell. He had ordered the sandwich from a nearby sub shop. The person who took his order didn't believe it was for real, and they never prepared the sandwich. He was forced to go to another shop that employed some people with disabilities, and they put a sandwich together for him on the spot.

As the OASIS sponsor, Craig and I had many opportunities to take Kirstin and her friends to conventions in various parts of Arizona. It was on one of those trips that we arrived at the hotel in Apache Junction with about twelve self-advocates in a fifteen-passenger van. The hotel clerk took pity on us when he saw our motley crew and upgraded Craig and me to a deluxe room on an upper floor that could only be accessed by using a special elevator key. After depositing our OASIS members safely in their rooms, we boldly took the elevator to our own little hideaway for a quiet night's sleep. Because the room came with a free continental breakfast, we also had the opportunity to sleep in a little. We kept reminding ourselves that these were adults, not high school students, and we weren't responsible for supervising twenty-four, seven.

Craig and I arrived at the opening session to find that none of our members was present. We were beginning to worry and thinking we needed to go find them when, to our relief, they came rushing in at the last minute. We could tell from Kirstin's expression that something had gone wrong, but we would have to wait until the break to find out what it was.

At the break, we nearly tripped over chairs to get to where they were sitting. Kirstin was obviously flustered and kept saying, "There wasn't anything we could do. We had to get to our meeting." When the whole story finally came out, we learned that they had all met at the restaurant for breakfast. They had no problems ordering their food, and everyone had time to eat. But by the time they finished, the restaurant was packed with people. Their server was very busy and was taking too long to get them their checks. They asked several times, but it was getting closer and closer to the time when they needed to get to their meeting. Finally, when they had just minutes left before the meeting started, they all got up and left without paying. Needless to say, Craig and I were horrified to hear that they had all skipped out on the bill. I'm sure they didn't realize that it was a type of stealing. To them, being late for the meeting was an even bigger crime. Craig was able to get with the hotel manager later and straighten it out.

Craig continued a fairly lucrative fund-raising activity that was started by Jean—selling Christmas wreaths. They were beautiful, fresh wreaths that we sold for $25 each. In the early years, we were able to make a good profit, but as shipping costs increased, the profits began to shrink. That was when Craig and Tom decided to drive up to Oregon to pick up the wreaths. I went with Craig on two of those trips, which involved marathon driving. We had to make the four thousand-mile round-trip in only three days. The profits from the wreath sale sustained the club for a year and meant they were able to do all their other projects.

Twice we were able to take the OASIS members who were the top wreath sellers to Disneyland. That was a little stressful, but mostly it was fun. Many of them had been to Disneyland before, but this was special, because they could go with their friends. We moved around Disneyland in a group, so no one got lost. I remember the first year that worked out fine—until we stopped to watch the fireworks. All of the lights were out so that the fireworks would show up better. When the show ended, it was very dark, with crowds of people moving around. When the lights came back on, Craig and I were standing alone. After a frightful half hour, we located everyone. On our next trip to Disneyland, we chose a meeting spot in case anyone became separated from the group.

Craig and I miss the days of OASIS meetings and conventions. The ARC was not able to sustain the local groups due to other financial obligations. We do have fond memories, however. OASIS provided much-needed opportunities for people with special needs to socialize with others in our state and to continue to grow as adults. It was also a way they could be recognized for their accomplishments as outstanding volunteers, workers, and self-advocates. Many of those awards went to members of Prescott OASIS, including Kirstin. Prescott OASIS was recognized as the outstanding self-advocacy group more than once. During the years she belonged to Prescott OASIS, Kirstin held every office, including president. That was a golden opportunity for her to further develop her communication and leadership skills.

Friends and acquaintances often say to us, "You must be so proud of Kirstin," and, of course, we tell them that we are. Very often this is followed up with them mentioning what a good job we have done. I have to agree with that as well. But the important word in that is "we." To acknowledge that "we" have done a good job is to recognize that neither of us could have done it alone. I have always been the one who set the standards for Kirstin and helped her face challenges, especially at school. However, the role Craig plays is equally as important. First of all, he has been a dad to Kirstin in every way. They love and cherish each other the way only fathers and daughters do. More than that, though, Craig has been present in her life in a very real way. He is the one who believes in Kirstin when I have doubts. It was Craig who helped Kirstin get her job at Costco and who drove her to work at four o'clock in the morning every workday. My coaching helped Kirstin earn her driving permit, but it will be Craig's determination that will help her reach a skill level to get a driver's license. While I have trouble picturing her driving by herself, he has no such nearsighted vision.

We are fortunate in our family to have a good support system. Michael and his family are always willing to help out. They support Kirstin in all of her efforts and are proud of her accomplishments. Because Michael grew up with a sister who had to work especially hard for what she wanted, he teaches his children to never give up when they face challenges. Our parents have always been devoted to Kirstin and believe in her ability to succeed. Her aunts, uncles, and cousins respect her as an adult and treat her that way. This extends to our friends and the members of our church, who see Kirstin as a shining example of what faith can accomplish. It is often said that it takes a village to raise a child. Kirstin has had the benefit of a truly outstanding one.

KIRSTIN'S SIDE OF THE STORY

I miss Prescott OASIS. I miss being with my friends and the parties we had. I liked the conventions. I learned a lot there. I'm glad I have Facebook, so I can keep track of my friends. I check my Facebook every day when I get home from work. I leave messages and send notes to my coworkers and friends. I have lots of friends all over Facebook, including my family.

It isn't easy being an adult. I am a registered voter, and I vote in every election. I am my own guardian. I handle my own finances. My parents give me some advice. I listen to them, but I make decisions for myself.

I do want to get married. I don't know how difficult marriage will be. I will support my husband any way I can. We decided not to have children. It is not easy to care for children. Having enough money is a pain in the rear. It will never go away. We just do the best we can.

Chapter Fourteen

ಶಾಡಿ

Angels Among Us

In February of 2009, Craig took a group of his OASIS members to the state capitol for Legislative Awareness Day, where they were able to meet their legislators, ask questions, and find out about the latest legislation affecting people with disabilities. In the afternoon, they sat in on a House session. Once in the chambers, they were invited down on the House floor by the representative from our area, Andy Tobin. After Andy's introduction, they received a standing ovation from the representatives. It occurred to me that we had come full circle from those early legislative hearings. These were not institutionalized adults, asking the legislature to allow them to live in the community. They were constituents, valuable members of society, adults deserving of recognition for their accomplishments.

In her book *Angel Unaware,* Dale Evans, whose child with Down syndrome only lived to be two years old, talked about how these special children were sent to earth for a purpose. For her daughter, that purpose was to wake them up to the need to live each day to the fullest and not focus so much on career success but on what is really important. I, too, believe these special people were sent to us for a purpose, but I think that purpose goes far beyond their immediate families and extends to everyone whose lives they touch. Ms. Evans took her title from Hebrews 13:2 (From The New American Bible. The New Catholic Translation. Catholic Bible Press. Copyright1987 by Thomas Nelson, Inc.), where we are reminded, "Do not neglect hospitality, for through it some have unknowingly entertained angels." I would add to that Matthew 25:40 (From The New American Bible. The New Catholic Translation. Catholic Bible Press. Copyright1987 by Thomas Nelson, Inc.): "Amen, I say to you, whatever you did for one of these least brothers of mine, you did for me." Clearly we have a directive to care for these most precious of our Father's children. For this we will receive blessings in this life and the next.

More than being our responsibility, I believe these angels who walk among us are our role models. Their lives are simple, and they are satisfied with what they are given. They care for others, even those who are not kind to them, without any expectation of reward. They are patient, gentle, and loving. They hold back nothing but share their feelings openly. They forgive and forget. I believe they are God's best work.

When Kirstin was about six years old, we went to visit Craig's aunt and uncle, Ray and Ila. Ila was a nurse, who cared for elderly patients in her home. We arrived at their house to find several seniors seated in chairs and wheelchairs in the living room. I wasn't sure what to do, but Kirstin wasted no time. One by one, she visited with each elderly person, taking their hands and talking softly to them. I was totally amazed by what she did, because it was so spontaneous and beautiful. The expressions on their faces changed from blank stares to tiny smiles.

Kirstin, and others like her, have a way of showing us all how we should live. One evening we were joining several of her friends at the food court at the mall. David was coming along with his mom, who was bringing someone else who lived in Prescott Valley. This was a person who was not very happy with Kirstin at the time and talked about her negatively to David all the way to the mall. By the time they arrived, David was angry and not speaking to Kirstin. David's mom filled me in on what was going on, and as usual, I became upset that someone would dare hurt my little girl. I continued to pout and even got up and left at one point.

When I returned to the food court, others had arrived. Kirstin was sitting there as if nothing had happened, even though David was still not talking to her. One of her friends is blind, and she asked for someone to help her order her food. Kirstin immediately volunteered. With a smile on her face, she helped her friend make her selections, order her food, and pay the clerk. Kirstin was the perfect example of Christian charity, and I, who displayed just the opposite type of behavior, was in awe of her. That night I learned a lesson I will always carry with me.

Every day, Kirstin touches lives in a very real way. A former general manager of Costco told me once that when she found herself stressed under the pressure of her job, she would go to the bakery and spend a few minutes with Kirstin. In total sincerity, Kirstin would put her arm around the manager's shoulder and say, "Let me sing you a song." Right on the spot, she would make up a song and sing it with no embarrassment to her manager. Who among us would be comfortable enough to do something like that? Certainly not me. I would be much too worried about what others might think.

Over the years, I have read many self-help books about how to get along in this world and how to influence others. I'm pretty sure that Kirstin hasn't read any. I recall some advice about the importance of remembering names. I've always been horrible at that, and I've only gotten worse as I've gotten older. Kirstin, on the other hand, could write her own book. Since she was a small child, she has made a point of learning names. I have watched her over and over when she meets someone for the first time. If the person is wearing a name tag, she reads the name out loud. Then she makes a comment about it. "I know someone with that same name." Or at the least, she says, "Nice name." If she can, she tries to associate that person with something or someone she knows. "You have the same hair color as Julia Roberts," or, "You look just like Randy Travis." I usually feel uncomfortable when she does this, especially if she tells the person he reminds her of John Candy. But Kirstin is doing it as a way of remembering, and in her mind, she is paying the person a compliment. In most cases, I'm sure it is taken that way. Kirstin's interest in others in genuine, and she makes an immediate connection.

Most of what I've learned about being a teacher I learned by being a teacher, not from teacher-training classes. But some of my skills I learned from Kirstin. She believes that we are all special in many ways, and I try to see my students as special. We all have flaws, but even the most difficult student has redeeming qualities. I've seen students with obnoxious behavior work lovingly and patiently with students who have more severe disabilities. I've had students ask me who the teacher's pet is. I tell them they all are. One year I had a student whose behaviors were obviously ones that would make it difficult for her to be well liked by the other students. I decided that for that year, I would treat her as if she were my favorite student. It was amazing how well it worked. Because my other students knew I liked her, they found her more likable as well. I'm not saying there weren't real problems, but she had friends that year, and maybe for the first time, she felt like she fit in. The year progressed, and near the end she asked me, "I'm your favorite student, aren't I?"

"You are," I told her. And she was.

I have often considered that if I were in charge of things in our country, there would never be a meeting of Congress or some big corporation without a person with Down syndrome present. Then those who are meeting would learn to listen to each other and treat each other with respect. They would not take themselves so seriously but would start caring more about other people. They would laugh more, and maybe they would even sing or dance. Maybe not as much work would get done, but whatever they did accomplish would be done right and would be best for all concerned. We have so much to learn from them, but most of us are too busy to even know it.

People with disabilities are making their marks in the world. Consider, for example, Nannie Marie Sanchez, whom Kirstin met at her OASIS convention. Although she has Down syndrome, Nannie is a well-known international speaker and a strong advocate for individuals with disabilities. When Nannie applied for admittance to her local community college, she was told that she was not eligible. Standing up for her rights, she insisted on being allowed to take the placement test and successfully passed the test for admittance. Nannie completed college, earning certification as a business administrative assistant. She then went on to run for a seat on the New Mexico Board of Education. She failed to get her party's nomination but made a good showing. She hosted her own television show, dealing with issues affecting people with disabilities. Today Ms. Sanchez operates a consulting business, assisting others with disabilities. She has aided in fund-raising projects in her state and monitors legislation involving people with special needs.

Every year, Kirstin and her friends march in the Alzheimer's Memory Walk. If given the chance at a microphone, each one of them will tell a story of why it is so important. Most have grandmothers, grandfathers, or other family members who have or have died from Alzheimer's. Even if they don't, they express their sincere need to help others. Their group is small compared to the large businesses with many employees who participate. And yet they are usually in the top five when it comes to raising money. And they walk ... the entire route, proudly carrying their banner. Their enthusiasm is contagious.

Workers at the local sheltered workshops volunteer regularly in their communities. They do jobs that no one else wants to do, like cleaning out the birdcages at a home for senior citizens. They call it paying back the community, because they recognize their lives are enriched by the help they receive from community groups. Every year there is a cleanup day for SNAP. This year they are cleaning a park around Willow Lake. For four hours, they will work to make the park clean and safe for others.

This reminded me of a time when a sorority I belonged to adopted a portion of the highway. We were responsible for keeping it clean. On our cleanup day, I took Kirstin, who was a teenager. As I walked along, picking up trash, I grumbled to myself about the irresponsible people who throw trash everywhere instead of disposing of it properly, as I do. After a while, I noticed Kirstin. She was saying things like, "Wow, I found a whole lot over here. Look, I hit the jackpot!" We had come out to clean up the trash. Why shouldn't we be excited about finding some? Eventually, we all adopted Kirstin's attitude, and the day went by much faster.

Certainly, Costco management knows what they are doing when, during fund-raising for the Children's Miracle Network, they strap a bucket around Kirstin's waist so she can receive donations while she works. Kirstin is happy to do it, because she knows it's a worthy cause. She is also happy to come to work an hour early dressed as a pirate to encourage donations as members come into shop. Kirstin is generous with her time, talent, and money. She has been a contributor to United Way since she began working at Costco.

Most people would agree that our most valuable resources are of the human variety. I wonder then why we are so willing to throw away people who don't quite fit in. The talented students I have seen pass through my classroom would astound and amaze most people. I had a student who began playing the piano at the age of three. He plays totally by ear and can play any music he hears. For those fortunate enough to hear him play, it is truly awesome. Another student has outstanding artistic ability. He draws with such detail, and his drawings are centered around scenarios that he creates. His interest in Civil War history led him to take that class in high school. There he was able to expand his interest in weaponry, and he created miniature versions of several weapons with full detail. He should be working as an animator or designer but will probably never have that opportunity. It will be our loss. Many of my students have artistic abilities that have won them awards, but most are not able to go further with their talents. I think of Kirstin, writing story after story that no one will ever read.

Most of my students are patient, helpful, loving people. They could serve as role models to the rest of us, but we push them away. It always amazes me when I go into a store and the clerk is rude and surly. What if someone else had that job, someone who smiled every day and treated people as if they were their instant friends? Wouldn't that be better than this? But all too often, people like that are passed over for employment, because they are a little slower or it takes them longer to learn something. Never mind that they will show up on time every day and will work as hard as they can to do a good job. Never mind that once they have learned the job, they will never forget it and will do it the same way every day. Never mind all of that, because they will never get the chance to show what they can do.

Nearly every day, I whine or complain about some small problem or some injustice I feel was done to me. I think we all do from time to time. If, for example, I had a cold sore or small blemish on my face, I might be focused on it, willing it to go away. Imagine being born with Sturge-Webber and having a port wine stain across half of your face. Though this may seem almost unbearable to us, those I know with the disorder have such charming smiles and twinkling eyes that soon the birthmark isn't noticeable at all.

One of the heroes from Arizona OASIS Conventions was a man named Bill Sackter. We never met Wild Bill, who died in 1983, but we did meet Thomas Walz, the author of his biography, *The Unlikely Celebrity*. Bill's life was the subject of a television movie titled *Bill*. It tells the story of Bill Sackter's life after he left the institution where he lived for forty-four years. The movie starred Mickey Rooney as Bill. Mickey Rooney received a Golden Globe for his portrayal. A sequel was made a few years later, and it was called *Bill on His Own*.

In the preface to his biography, Bill explains, "Tom seemed to think I was really some buddy special, like one of God's chosen or somethin'. If he wants to think that way, ain't nothin' I can do. But so's you know, I wass ally jus a crack-minded person who found me a different world by lookin' to its happy side instead of its bad side. I learned that what you see is what you is, and I was tired of bad things happenin' to me. all I wants is the good things not—lotsa frens, a good sandwiches in my lunch box, some polka music, and maybe even a big sicar from ol John. Also, I'd like a beer now and then."

Born in Minneapolis in 1913, Bill was the fourth child of an immigrant couple named Sam and Mary Sackter. When he was seven years old, he was placed in the State School for the Feeble Minded and Epileptics. There he remained until, in the 1960s, a movement to deinstitutionalize mental health facilities left him roaming the streets of Minneapolis on his own. Eventually, he was taken in by a young couple who petitioned for and was granted guardianship of Bill. Later, when his guardian became the director of the University of Iowa's School of Social Work, Bill moved there, too, and got a job at the university as well. Bill became the owner of Wild Bill's Coffee Shop on the university campus.

Bill was a boarder at Mae Driscoll's, where he shared a home with other people with cognitive challenges. The neighbors never complained about her unusual boarders or the fact that Bill liked to sit on the front porch and play polka music on his harmonica.

During his lifetime, Bill received countless awards, including Iowa's Handicapped Citizen of the Year and a Presidential Award from the American Academy of Cerebral Palsy. He played Santa to hospitalized children and played his harmonica at concerts. The ARC has a research center named the Bill Sackter Center for Self-Determination, and in Iowa, there is a Bill Sackter Harmonica Festival. Wild Bill's Coffee Shop continues as a service-learning site at the University of Iowa.

Such a simple life, a life that was thrown away, and yet Bill's contributions are far-reaching. To those who knew Bill, he gave so much in the way of kindness, gentleness, and a sense of humor that drew people to him. His simple views on life taught each person something about himself or herself. He truly was a gift from God.

In today's fast-paced world, where our lives are complicated and we have very little time for ourselves, let alone others, it is refreshing to know people who aren't caught up in the frenzy—people who still take time to talk, smile, and laugh. When I see a family with a child who has a disability, I never feel pity for them. Instead, I feel joy at knowing that they are blessed in so many ways. With all the demands that are placed on those families, there are also many rewards. There are moments of accomplishment that will mean more to them because of the price they have to pay for those accomplishments.

As Catholic Christians, we believe deeply in the act of contrition. We take seriously the part of the Lord's Prayer where we say, "Forgive us our trespasses as we forgive those who trespass against us." Forgiveness is an absolute necessity in our faith. In fact, we are not able to participate at the Lord's table if we are holding onto any anger or resentment toward one another. How much Kirstin understands of that I'm not sure, but when it comes to putting it into practice, she is unwavering. If she feels she has wronged anyone, she goes immediately to that person and makes amends. I know firsthand the peace that comes from being unburdened of sin. And yet there are times when I hold onto my anger, refusing to let it go and carrying it like a weight tied round my waist. I have never seen Kirstin do that, even when she might be justified in doing so. She asks for forgiveness and offers forgiveness as if it were as natural to her as breathing.

I was trying to share with Kirstin that when we worry, we are calling Jesus a liar, because He has promised to provide for all our needs. After the third attempt, I gave up, because all Kirstin was hearing was me calling Jesus a liar. Later, I realized that Kirstin doesn't really worry. She uses that term, and she will say that she is worried about something, but she doesn't worry the way I do. Kirstin might worry about getting her work done if she only has thirty minutes left before her shift is over and she still has lots to do. She would never worry about getting her work done tomorrow. It would never occur to her to worry about that. I'm convinced that Kirstin would get the same good night's sleep if she were facing an IRS audit or going to Disneyland. Worrying about future things is not something she would waste time or energy on.

When I pray, I am often praising God or thanking Him. Many times, I am asking for things I need. I call Jesus my friend, but I rarely have a heart-to-heart talk with Him. I wonder at someone like Bill Sackter, who talked to God every day as if He were right there with him. Bill reasoned that since God is so busy, He probably doesn't have much time to watch TV or see movies. So Bill would tell Him about a TV show or movie he had seen, just in case God missed it. How simple and innocent that seems, but also what an intimate relationship Bill had with his Lord. I wonder if this is what Jesus meant when He told us to come to Him as little children.

Looking back on our lives, it seems we have come so far. Those limited expectations I had when Kirstin was diagnosed with Down syndrome are long gone. Now I see a world not with limitations but only with possibilities and challenges for the future. What will that future hold for children born today with developmental delays? I can't even speculate. For my family, helping Kirstin grow into an independent woman is only the beginning. My niece, Andrea, is a special education teacher. She started as an aide while she was still working on her degree. I remember her first visit after she took that position. She spoke with such warmth and enthusiasm about her students, telling a little about each one. I knew then that she had been bitten by the bug, and her life would never be the same. I saw the same thing happen when my granddaughter, Brenna, began working with the special education class at her middle school. It was obvious she had been bitten by the same bug.

Throughout most of her life, Kirstin has walked a thin line between the world of those with developmental challenges and the world the rest of us live in. Over the years, that line has become blurred, and more often, Kirstin has chosen our world over the simpler, safer world that could be hers. As Christians, one of our greatest challenges is to live in the world and not become of the world. I have struggled with that all of my life. Even now, as I finish this work, I can't help but wonder how my life will be changed by it. Will I claim it as my own accomplishment, or will I recognize it as coming from the hand of the One who made me? One thing I do know: I will have a beacon of light to follow, a bright and shining ray to guide me on my way to discovering God's grace.

KIRSTIN'S SIDE OF THE STORY

I read the book by Dale Evans. I was crying when I read about Dale's child with Down syndrome. I was sorry that she died. I know she is happy in heaven. I think she is looking down on me right now. She is helping us who have Down syndrome.

I do understand how the elderly people feel. I do care about them. I know from experience because I live with a senior, my grandmother. Always remember the good times you have with your grandmother and grandfather. You will not always have them.

We are all angels in this world. We all should care. We all should love. We all have feelings. We all should forgive. Talk about your problems with others who have experiences like you. Control your anger with other people. We all have heroes. We all need someone to look up to. I like to collect biographies about my heroes.

We need to keep our earth clean. That way we will have a place to live and grow up. We all have to do our part.

We all wish to be normal in this world. We all have talents. I can write stories if my mom trusts me with it. We all need to believe in ourselves. We should help each other do our best. That will be our greatest reward.

Bibliography

Rogers, Dale Evans, *Angel Unaware*. Grand Rapids, MI: Fleming H. Revell, 1953.

US Bureau of Labor Statistics, *Data on the Employment Status of People with a Disability*. Washington DC: Division of Labor Force Statistics, 2010. http://data.bls.gov (accessed July 30, 2011).

US Equal Employment Opportunity Commission, "Chuck E. Cheese's Must Pay Maximum Damages Under Multi-million Dollar Jury Award." Washington DC: EEOC, 2000. http://www1.eeoc.gov//eeoc/newroom/release/3-15-00.cfm (accessed July 5, 2011).

Walz, Thomas, *The Unlikely Celebrity*. Carbondale: Southern Illinois University Press, 1998.

About the Authors

Rosemary Heddens has been a special education teacher at Bradshaw Mountain High for the past twenty-nine years. She is a graduate of Arizona State University with a BA in secondary education and an MA in special education. She lives with her husband, Craig, in Chino Valley, Arizona. Together, they enjoy hiking the forested trails near their home and kayaking on the picturesque lakes.

Kirstin Heddens is beginning her fourteenth year as a worker in the Costco store in Prescott, Arizona. She is a graduate of Bradshaw Mountain High School. Kirstin lives in her own home in Prescott. She plays chimes at the American Evangelical Lutheran Church.

CPSIA information can be obtained
at www.ICGtesting.com
Printed in the USA
LVHW112148090320
649543LV00001B/192